KT-486-634

York St John College
Fountains Learning Cer

Please return

10 JUN 2024

York St. John College

3 8025 00481613 1

NANCY
NELSON

— PEOPLE TO KNOW —

Steven Spielberg
Hollywood Filmmaker

YORK ST. JOHN
COLLEGE LIBRARY

Virginia Meachum

Enslow Publishers, Inc.

40 Industrial Road   PO Box 38
Box 398   Aldershot
Berkeley Heights, NJ 07922   Hants GU12 6BP
USA   UK

http://www.enslow.com

Copyright ©1996 by Virginia Meachum

All rights reserved.

No part of this book may be reproduced by any means
without the written permission of the publisher.

Library of Congress Cataloging-in-Publication Data

Meachum, Virginia.
    Steven Spielberg: Hollywood filmmaker / Virginia Meachum.
        p. cm. — (People to know)
    Filmography: p.
    Includes bibliographical references and index.
    Summary: Explores the life and career of the successful filmmaker beginning
with his childhood and including discussion of his projects as a director, writer,
and producer.
    ISBN 0-89490-697-6
    1. Spielberg, Steven, 1947–   —Juvenile literature. 2. Motion picture
producers and directors—United States—Biography—Juvenile literature.
[1. Spielberg, Steven, 1947–   .] I. Title. II. Series.
PN1998.3.S65M43   1996
791.43'0233'092—dc20   95-39022
                                                            CIP
                                                            AC

Printed in the United States of America

10 9 8 7 6

Illustration Credits:
Academy of Motion Picture Arts and Sciences, pp. 4, 76, 99; AP/Wide
World Photos, p. 102; Everett Collection, pp. 26, 35, 39, 43, 51, 54, 62,
66, 79, 83, 88, 96; John Trotto, p. 18.

Cover Illustration: Everett Collection

Contents

Director Steven Spielberg is awarded two Oscars—for Best Director and Best Picture—at the 1993/66th Annual Academy Awards.

And the Oscar Goes to . . .

At the Los Angeles Music Center, hundreds of excited movie fans are crowded onto bleachers outside the Dorothy Chandler Pavilion. Their wild cheers and applause greet Hollywood's top stars, who are emerging from gleaming stretch limousines onto the red-carpeted runway. Inside, on this night of March 21, 1994, the sixty-sixth Academy Awards ceremony will soon take place.

Each year, the Academy of Motion Picture Arts and Sciences (AMPAS) presents awards of merit for distinctive achievement in the film industry. The award is a golden statuette nicknamed Oscar. The Oscar, a symbol of professional success, is the most popular and prestigious award in the film world.[1]

Membership in the Academy, which was founded in

1927, is by invitation only, with members divided into thirteen branches. To select nominees for awards, each branch may choose five nominees from within its category. For example, actors nominate actors, directors nominate directors, and writers nominate writers. For the Best Picture category, the entire membership may submit nominations. Then the members (currently about five thousand) vote on the nominees by secret ballot.

Price, Waterhouse and Company, a firm of certified public accountants, counts the votes in each category to determine the winners. Each winner's name is placed in an envelope, which is then sealed. The envelope remains sealed, and the name is a secret, until the envelope is opened at the televised Academy Awards ceremony in the spring. On being announced, each winner is called to the platform to receive an Oscar. Tonight, Oscars will be awarded in twenty-three categories of achievement, with those for Best Actor, Best Actress, Best Director, and Best Picture creating worldwide curiosity and suspense.

Among the celebrities arriving is Steven Spielberg, accompanied by his wife, Kate Capshaw, and his mother, Leah Adler. As the director of such popular films as *Jaws*, *Close Encounters of the Third Kind*, and *E.T.: The Extra-Terrestrial*, Spielberg has been a nominee four times, but never a winner.

For the nominees, this is an evening of honor, but also of suspense. Each has a chance to win "Best" in his or her category. Who will it be? Walking briskly toward the Pavilion, the arriving stars are followed by a swarm of media reporters and photographers. "How do you feel?" Spielberg is asked by ABC's television reporter Joel Siegel. "Nervous," he replies, a smile visible within his trim beard. His next words fade into the surrounding din, but "my chattering teeth" can be faintly heard.[2]

On this night, Spielberg has been nominated for Best Director, and the film he has produced and directed, *Schindler's List*, has received the nomination for Best Picture. Adapted from the book by Thomas Keneally, *Schindler's List* presents the true story of a German industrialist who saved more than one thousand Jews from the horrors of Nazi death camps during World War II. Described by moviegoers as "haunting" and "powerful," this black-and-white film has received overwhelmingly favorable reviews by critics.

Another of Spielberg's films, *Jurassic Park*, is a nominee in three other catagories—Visual Effects, Sound, and Sound Editing. Based on the best-selling novel by Michael Crichton, the film is set in a theme park featuring real dinosaurs brought back to life. During a power outage, Tyrannosaurus rex goes on a rampage of heart-stopping terror. A box-office success, this film has been heralded for its riveting suspense and astonishing special effects.

Now seated inside among the other celebrities, Spielberg, in tuxedo and black tie, blends in with everybody else. As a boy, he had yearned desperately to be like everybody else. Sensitive about his Jewish heritage, he longed to be accepted by his non-Jewish friends—to be like the other kids in his neighborhood. Now, the forty-six-year-old director gives little thought to being like anyone but himself. For more than twenty years, he has been immersed in what he likes to do best—making movies. His imagination, technical skill, and creativity have resulted in an astounding number of feature films and TV programs. Even though his films are popular with moviegoers throughout the world, some critics in the movie industry have looked upon his work as having more fantasy than substance.

Hosted by Whoopi Goldberg, a former Oscar winner as Best Supporting Actress in *Ghost*, the lengthy program tonight moves entertainingly through musical numbers, film clips of performances by nominees, and Oscar presentations in the various categories. Meanwhile, tension is building toward the announcement of awards in the final categories.

At last, film clips are shown from the five Best Director nominees. Each receives well-deserved applause. A hush settles over the vast audience. The presenter, Clint Eastwood, who was awarded Best Director last year, rips open a sealed envelope and announces to all, "The Oscar goes to Steven Spielberg for *Schindler's List!*"[3]

Surrounded by applause and words of congratulation, the smiling honoree strides toward the platform to accept his award. Shortly afterward, when Best Picture of the Year is announced, Spielberg's film *Schindler's List* is pronounced the winner of that award, too.

Suddenly, in this shining moment, a golden Oscar in each hand, the boy who wanted to be "like everybody else" is the Best Director—of the Best Picture—like nobody else!

Growing Pains

Steven Spielberg began wanting to be like everybody else soon after his family moved from an all-Jewish neighborhood in Cincinnati, Ohio, to Haddonfield, New Jersey, a community in which few Jews lived. As he grew up, he very much wanted to be like the other kids—to fit in. "Being a Jew meant that I was not normal. I was not like everybody else," Spielberg says, recalling those early years. "I just wanted to be accepted. Not for who I was. I wanted to be accepted for who everybody else was."[1]

This difference particularly bothered him during the Christmas season. Throughout the neighborhood, homes glittered with lighted wreaths and trees. Reindeer and Santas glowed from rooftops and doorways. The Spielberg home was noticeably dark. Steven, now age seven, begged his parents to add Christmas lights like everybody else, but they explained that Jews did not put up lights at Christmas. His father suggested instead that they place a menorah in the window. This nine-branched candelabrum celebrates Chanukah, the Jewish Festival of Lights.

"*No! No! No!*" cried Steven. "People will think we're Jewish."[2] Steven's parents were accustomed to the religious differences between themselves and their neighbors. They had both been raised in Orthodox Jewish homes in which the traditional beliefs and practices of Judaism were strictly followed. This included study of the Torah, and strict observance of the Sabbath, festivals, and dietary laws (the laws of Judaism that are about preparing and eating food).[3] Although Steven's parents followed Jewish tradition less strictly than their own parents had done, they lit candles each Friday at sundown for the Sabbath, and celebrated the Jewish holidays. The Sabbath, a holy day for Jews, begins each Friday before sunset and ends after sundown on Saturday, during which time many Jews attend services in a synagogue or temple.[4] Whenever Steven's grandparents came for lengthy visits, Yiddish (a common language of Jewish immigrants from Eastern Europe) was spoken, and the hours were filled with stories about Austria and Russia, where family members had once lived.[5]

Steven's father, Arnold Spielberg, was an electrical

engineer. As part of a team that designed the first computer, he soon would become recognized as an expert in this new area of electronic technology.

Steven's mother, Leah Posner, was a former concert pianist. Creative and energetic, she would often gather musician friends in her home in order to play chamber concerts. Their first child, and only son, Steven Alan Spielberg, was born on December 18, 1947, in Cincinnati, Ohio. In the following years, they had three daughters—Anne, Sue, and Nancy.

Although Leah and Arnold Spielberg had widely different interests—hers in music and his in technology—they both loved their children and were responsible, caring parents. In the 1950s, television had become popular home entertainment, but young Steven was easily frightened by things he saw on TV.[6] Once, a documentary on snakes left him crying for hours. From then on, Leah and Arnold strictly rationed their children's viewing, limiting it mostly to shows like *The Mickey Mouse Club*, cartoons, and other children's programs.

At about the age of five, Steven was taken to his first movie, *The Greatest Show on Earth*, a circus spectacular produced by Cecil B. DeMille. Steven was captivated by the feeling of being drawn into the action that was taking place on the big screen. This may have sparked his interest in entertaining. Before long, his active imagination led him to create stories, both funny and scary, which he dramatized in puppet shows for his young sisters and their friends. He seemed to enjoy making his audience react with laughter or wonder.

Skinny, sensitive, and unathletic, Steven was not drawn toward outdoor sports. Although he was pleased to be included in neighborhood football games, he was always afraid that his clumsiness would show.[7] His bedroom was the place where he made his great escapes, spending increasing amounts of time with the door closed. The door was closed because of several pet parakeets, a gift from his parents, that flew freely about the room. Steven named them all Shmuck, a name he liked.[8] Then, numbering them I, II, III, and IV, he trained them to perch on the curtain rod.

In this room, amid a clutter of toys, toy trains, and assorted other objects, his imagination went to work. Ghosts hid in the closet, creepy-crawlies lurked under his bed, and little people lived inside a crack in the wall. At night, the trees outside his window became grotesque figures with heads and arms and tentacles. In contrast to his early fear of television characters, Steven grew to like the sensation of being scared; "as a kid I liked pushing myself to the brink of terror and then pulling back," he admitted years later.[9] Steven liked to scare his sisters, too. Sue, five years younger than her brother, recalls:

> When he was babysitting for us, he'd resort to creative torture. One time he came into the bedroom with his face wrapped in toilet paper like

a mummy. He peeled off the paper layer by layer and threw it at us. He was a delight, but a terror. And we kept coming back for more.[10]

Another of their brother's creations was the story he told of a wartime flier's body rotting in one of the family's closets. Devising a makeshift head from a plastic skull topped with his father's World War II aviator cap and goggles, Steven dared his little sisters to enter the dark closet. Once they were inside, he closed the door. Then, with a rigged-up device, he lighted the skull from outside, causing instant screams of terror. Says Steven, "It's amazing that I grew up and they didn't kill me."[11]

Due to Arnold Spielberg's expertise in the fast-growing computer industry, his work took him and his family to Phoenix, Arizona, in 1956, where they settled in the suburb of Scottsdale. Steven was nine. As a newcomer in another community where few Jews lived, he tried once again to fit in—to be like everybody else. He participated in Little League®, played his clarinet in the school band, and marched in local parades. At age twelve, he became acquainted with home movies. This opened up a whole new area of interest.

In 1960, Steven's mother gave his father an eight-millimeter Kodak camera for Father's Day. (Film used for home movies is generally eight or sixteen millimeters wide, which is one fourth or one half the size of standard movie film. Professional film is thirty-five millimeters wide.) Steven soon learned to operate the camera, began taking movies of family events, and was granted permission to become the official family photographer. From then on, camping trips and other family activities would never be the same. With Steven's creative spirit, each event recorded by the camera was dramatized. Lighting, setting, and action were all directed by the young photographer—with parents and sisters playing their roles. Says Spielberg, "My Dad had to wait for me to say 'Action!' before he could put the knife into the fish to clean it."[12] His talent for directing had begun to emerge.

Fascinated with this new hobby, Steven spent hours in his own private world plotting stories, setting up scenes, and filming from different angles. He had joined a Boy Scout troop, and he was determined to earn a merit badge in photography. He did—with a three-minute movie called *Gunsmog* (named after *Gunsmoke*, a TV cowboy show). Filmed in the nearby desert, with his fellow Scouts as actors, it featured a stagecoach holdup, a sheriff, and a bad guy (actually, a dummy made of clothes, pillows, and shoes) who plunged off a cliff.[13] Earning the merit badge boosted his confidence, and he continued to work on technique—not only setting up shots and filming, but learning to edit, taking pieces of film shot at different times and making them into one film.

Steven had never been fond of school, and this consuming project began to take the time he needed for studying. Arnold Spielberg, a "hardworking perfectionist," tolerated his son's obsessive moviemaking as long as his grades were satisfactory.[14] When Arnold was home (less and less often, partly because of his work), he spent many hours helping Steven with math, a subject that was particularly troublesome.

Steven's mother was totally receptive to her son's creativity. Leah explained:

> He was my first, so I didn't know that everybody didn't have kids like him. Our living room was strewn with cables and floodlights—that's where Steven did his filming. We never said no. We never had a chance to say no. Steven didn't understand that word.[15]

Steven obviously had won the good-humored support of his mother and sisters. His father supported him, too. When he was home, he would help construct movie sets with toy trucks and papier-mâché mountains. This family support shines through in an incident that Steven's youngest sister, Nancy, relates about playing a role in one of his films when she was eight years old. When she was supposed to reach up toward the "firelight," Steven had her look directly at the sun. "'Don't blink!'" he'd shout. "And though I might have gone blind, I did what he said because, after all, it was Steven directing."[16]

To raise money to buy film for these movies, Steven often turned the living room into a mini-theater, showing his own movies or rented ones. His mother and sisters helped by making popcorn. The first time he did this, he made $36. Instead of buying film, however, he donated his profit to a local school for the handicapped. Sensitive to those less fortunate than himself, Steven once deliberately fell in a school race to allow a mentally disabled boy to cross the line ahead of him. The other boys cheered and laughed at his defeat, and he later remarked, "I'd never felt better and I'd never felt worse in my entire life."[17]

At Phoenix Arcadia High School, Steven joined the theater arts program, but school was not a priority in his life. He already knew that he wanted to be a movie director, and he could not understand why science, math, and foreign languages were important. Besides, he never felt comfortable among his classmates. "At school I felt like a real nerd, the skinny, acne-faced wimp who gets picked on by big football jocks all the way home. . . ."[18]

His sister Anne, two years younger than he, remembers things differently. "He had more friends than he remembers having." Referring to a picture of him back then, she says:

> Yes, there's a nerd. There's the crewcut . . . the ears . . . the skinny body. But he really had an incredible personality. He could make people do things. He made everything he was going to do sound like you wished you were part of it.[19]

He did get people to do things, recruiting his family,

Steven Spielberg attended Phoenix Arcadia High School in Arizona.

friends, and even the school bully (who had given him grief all year long) to play roles in his eight-millimeter movies. They served as actors, costume and makeup artists, writers, and set designers. With this makeshift production company, he made a whole series of mini-movies, including war movies, Westerns, and science fiction movies.

Battle Squad was the film in which Steven cast the fourteen-year-old who had been giving him a hard time at school. The plot involved fighting the Nazis. The bully played the role of a Nazi squad leader, complete with helmet, fatigues, and backpack. After appearing in this film, Steven's former worst enemy became his new best friend.

In 1960, Steven won a contest for his war movie *Escape to Nowhere*. *Firelight* was the title of the most ambitious film Steven made while he was in high school. This two-and-a-half-hour science fiction epic centered around a team of scientists who were investigating mysterious lights appearing in the night sky. Steven's father rented a Phoenix theater for a one-night showing. The film had cost $400 to make, and netted a profit of $100. It was Steven Spielberg's first box-office success.

In 1964, Arnold Spielberg's work required that the family move to Saratoga, California, a suburb of San Jose. Once again Steven needed to adjust to a new territory, another school, other teenagers. As a transfer student entering an unfamiliar high school in his senior year, Steven was not warmly welcomed by some of the other students. Here again, not being "like everybody else," he became a target for anti-Semitic bullies. The anti-Semites would call out, "Hey, Jew!" then strike him physically. In study hall, the same students threw pennies at him. "Pick them up, Jew," they taunted. Steven remembers the sound of those pennies landing around his desk: "in that quiet study hall every penny sounded like the explosion of a bazooka."[20] Steven endured the abuse, determined just to get through this final year.

Meanwhile, things at home had not been going well either. For several years, Steven and his sisters had been aware of their parents' unhappiness with each other. The sound of their arguing at night, and their talk of divorce, seeped through the heating ducts and into the children's bedrooms. By now, the clashing of their personalities had reached a climax. Leah and Arnold Spielberg separated. They divorced in 1965. To young Steven, the word "divorce" was an ugly one. He did not feel he had a father anymore.[21] Steven graduated from high school in June 1965; it had not been a very good year.

Focus on Film

The summer after graduation, when Spielberg visited cousins who lived near Los Angeles, California, he took a Universal Studios tour and was immediately caught up in the excitement of seeing a real studio. He wanted to see even more than the tour offered. During a rest stop, Spielberg left the group to look around. In his unofficial wandering, he accidentally came upon and was questioned by Chuck Silvers, head of Universal's editorial department. Instead of calling the guards, he listened to Spielberg, who spoke about his own filmmaking. Curious, Silvers gave him a pass to return the next day with his films. After viewing Spielberg's work, Silvers said he was impressed, but could do no more for him—not even give him a pass to return to the Universal lot.

Spielberg was not easily deterred. The next day, wearing a business suit, carrying a briefcase, and giving a friendly wave to the unsuspecting gate attendant, he walked briskly past and onto the Universal lot. He did this five days a week all through the summer. The attendant probably mistook him for a son of one of the studio executives.

Spielberg's boldness provided him with a unique learning opportunity. Since no one questioned his presence, he found an office that was not being used, bought a plastic name plate, and inserted his name and office number in the building directory. He soon became familiar on the lot, hanging out with film editors, writers, and other studio personnel. Actually, Spielberg wanted to observe the shooting of a film on a sound stage, but no unofficial visitors were allowed. One day, he did manage to get onto director Alfred Hitchcock's set for *Torn Curtain*, but he was soon discovered and was hastily evicted by an assistant director.[1] However, by listening to the professional moviemakers and observing activities on the studio lot, he learned much about the industry. He also tried to get someone else to look at his films, but with no success.

During the following two years, he continued to write stories and to create his own movies. He wanted to get into a major film school like that in the University of Southern California or the University of California at Los Angeles, but his high school grades were not high enough. In the fall of 1967, Spielberg enrolled at California State University at Long Beach. The university did not have a film school, so he majored in English. He was determined to pursue a career in film, however. Arranging to cram his classes into a two-day-a-week schedule, he spent his other days attending movies, making his own eight-millimeter movies, and persisting in asking studio executives to view his work. No one wanted anything he had to offer; he was told that if he would make his films on sixteen- or, even better, thirty-five-millimeter film, they would get seen.

Steven went to work in the college cafeteria to earn enough money to buy film and to rent a sixteen-millimeter camera. He was determined to show studio executives what he could do with a camera if he had a chance, but he proved to be unsuccessful in getting a showing for even this work.

Meanwhile, Spielberg was meeting other students with filmmaking careers in mind. Among them were Dennis Hoffman, a wealthy young man who hoped to become a professional producer, and Allen Daviau, who was studying photography. With the financial backing of Hoffman, and camera assistance from Daviau, Spielberg made a twenty-two-minute film called *Amblin'* in 1968. It is the story of a young man and young woman who fall in love—without exchanging any words—while hitchhiking from the Mojave desert to the Pacific coast. Actually, it was shot in Palm Desert, California, in ten days, and cost $10,000 to produce. They held a screening that was well attended by people in the film industry, but brought no one interested in promoting *Amblin'.*

Once again Spielberg managed to get the film into the hands of Chuck Silvers on the Universal lot. Silvers, who remembered the young film enthusiast from two summers earlier, viewed *Amblin'* and was impressed enough to ask Sidney Jay Sheinberg, who was then head of Universal's TV production, to look at it.

"So I watched it and I thought it was terrific," Sheinberg recalls. "I liked the way he selected the performers, the relationships, the maturity and the warmth that was in that short."[2] He asked that Spielberg come to see him. When Spielberg appeared on the following day in 1969, Sheinberg offered him a seven-year contract to direct television series for Universal. Says Spielberg, "I quit college so fast I didn't even clean out my locker."[3]

At last, Steven Spielberg's perseverance and his belief in himself were bringing positive results. The Universal executives, however, were not the only ones to appreciate *Amblin'.* In 1969, it won awards at both the Venice and Atlanta film festivals, and was paired with *Love Story* for national distribution the following year.

At age twenty-one, Spielberg had become the youngest director in the studio's history. His first assignment was an episode of Rod Serling's *Night Gallery* series called "Eyes." This is the story of a wealthy blind woman who schemes to buy temporary eyesight. Academy Award winner and longtime Hollywood star Joan Crawford was to play the leading role. To direct so legendary an actress on his first assignment was a scary prospect. Spielberg later described it as "a very traumatic experience," although he spoke highly of Crawford, describing her as the only person on the crew who treated him as if he already had been working for fifty years. "She was terrific, totally professional. She relied on me to direct her more than I ever thought she would."[4]

He went on to direct other series for NBC, including episodes of *Marcus Welby, M.D., The Psychiatrists, The Name of the Game, Owen Marshall,* and *Columbo.* For two years, he improved his camera technique and polished his skill at directing actors, but his work was limited to routine television assignments.

In 1971, after two years of successful series directing, Spielberg was given his first chance at a feature-length film. *Duel,* based on a short story written by Richard Matheson for *Playboy* magazine, was to be a television movie-of-the-week. In this terrifying thriller, a traveling salesman is relentlessly pursued by an unseen driver in a highly flammable tank truck. The action takes place along a remote highway, and goes on suspensefully for almost ninety minutes, until the distraught salesman eventually outwits the homicidal trucker.

Actor Dennis Weaver was cast as the mild-mannered salesman. The other major character to be cast was the

Dennis Weaver, as a traveling salesman in *Duel*, is pursued by an unseen driver in a monstrous truck. A television movie-of-the-week, this was Spielberg's first feature film.

truck. From a lineup of nearly a dozen semis, Spielberg and his production staff chose one that, with some remodeling, could be made to look both human and sinister. Two hydraulic tanks were added to each side of the doors, to suggest the truck's ears. Dead grasshoppers were scattered on the grill, and dead bugs were spread over the windshield to make seeing the driver more difficult. Next, the truck was given a bubble bath of motor oil and chunky black and crud-brown paint:

> It layered, bubbled, and pocked in the sun and eventually hardened. That was its makeup. . . . Then we added a half dozen license plates so you would perhaps assume that this truck had dueled with many cars across six to eight states.[5]

In the movie, the salesman's car passes a truck on the highway, and the truck becomes menacing as it speeds up and forces him off the road. When the shaken salesman resumes his journey, the truck reappears behind him in pursuit. Throughout segments of the film, the salesman is forced to drive for his life at heart-pounding speed. Spielberg explained how he captured the feeling of this incredible speed on camera:

> We had a camera car. It was a made-over Corvette with the fiberglass body removed and the cameras mounted very, very low, three to four inches off the ground. Just by being low to the ground you get an amazing sense of speed and velocity—you can't get that sense from up high looking down, only from low gazing up.[6]

The filming was finished in only sixteen days, but it ended up being two and a half hours long, much too long for a television movie. It had to be reduced to one hour and fifteen minutes. So Spielberg began the tedious process of cutting, editing, correcting the color, and adding the music composed by Billy Goldenberg.

Viewer response to *Duel* was so positive that in 1973, the movie was released for theater showing in Europe, Japan, and Australia. It won awards at film festivals in Monaco, Italy, and West Germany. Well-known director David Lean (director of *A Passage to India*) had seen Spielberg's television movie *Duel* as a theatrical feature in Europe, and he knew immediately that here was a very bright new director. "Steven takes real pleasure in the sensuality of forming action scenes—wonderful flowing movements. . . . But then Steven is the way the movies used to be. He just loves making films."[7]

The following year, Spielberg made two more feature movies for television, *Something Evil* and *Savage*. Although less successful than *Duel*, they were generally well received. With his camera tricks and frightening visual effects, he had begun to establish a reputation as a master of suspense.

Now he was being flooded with film offers, but found none to his liking. He was ready to try something else.

A Breakthrough

Now that the success of *Duel* had established Spielberg as a promising director of feature-length films, he wanted to do something of his own choice—something more personal. While thinking about this, he rediscovered a 1969 newspaper clipping that told of a young couple's desperate attempt to recapture their child from a foster home in Sugarland, Texas. He thought this was an appealing human interest story on which to base a feature film.

Taking time off from his television directing, Spielberg wrote his own screenplay, developing it into a comedy-drama. He then engaged two young writers, Hal Barwood and Matthew Robbins, whom he had met at a USC film school exhibit, to tighten up the script. Spielberg was now twenty-five, and this would be his first attempt at directing an original theatrical movie for Universal. *Duel, Savage,* and *Something Evil* all had been made for television. When he presented his script for *The Sugarland Express* to the studio executives, they said, "We'll let you make this movie, but first you have to get a producer who knows how to produce—we don't want to trust you with the producing chores."[1] (The producer is the person who agrees to finance the making of a movie. If more than one person accepts this responsibility, they all are called coproducers.) Upon reading the script, producers Richard Zanuck and David Brown agreed to provide the financing for *The Sugarland Express,* with Spielberg as the director.

Few people sitting in a movie theater are aware of the kind of work that goes into making a movie, especially the preproduction time, before filming. Most moviemakers start as Spielberg did, with an idea for a story. The idea may come from a novel that has been purchased by the studio, from a play, a biography, a news item, the story department of the studio, or from other sources.

The idea is then developed into a story with a plot, and turned over to a scriptwriter, who creates the dialogue to be spoken by the actors, and indicates the action in each camera shot or scene. Also included are descriptions of the background or setting for each shot, and instructions about the photography.

Once a screenplay or script is read and accepted by a

producer, a director is chosen. The producer and director become a team, developing a budget and a shooting schedule, estimating how much the entire project will cost and how long the shooting should take.

For *The Sugarland Express*, Spielberg had written the story with the idea that he would be the one directing it. Now that he had the necessary financial backing by coproducers Zanuck and Brown, the three would become a team, developing a budget and a shooting schedule—estimating how much the filming would cost and how long the shooting should take. As director, Spielberg needed to be in on every stage of the planning, including the hiring of a crew to carry out his overall vision of the film. A production manager, directors of photography, art, costume design, makeup, editing, and a technical staff are all essential to develop a plan of action for turning the script into an actual movie. For his cinematographer, the director of photography, Spielberg chose Vilmos Zsigmond, whose camerawork had impressed him in past films. Other crew members who had experience in particular areas of filmmaking were soon added.

Selecting a cast is another vital step in the preproduction period. The producers of *The Sugarland Express* were anxious about Spielberg directing his first feature without a well-known star in the leading role, so he interviewed several possible movie stars, none of whom were interested in the role. Then Spielberg thought of Goldie Hawn, who was well known for her television work in *Laugh-In*, a comedy show, and had won an Academy Award for Best Supporting Actress in *Cactus Flower* in 1968. He met with her and was pleased with the results. "She understood the script, she understood the role. Most of her relatives came from Texas, so she could do the accent without much effort."[2] The studio was pleased, too, even though, as Spielberg relates:

> Of course, she cost more than all the police cars and a lot of the other production values. I made the picture for about $2 million, and out of that $300,000 was Goldie's salary. Today that's a low figure for a star. In 1973 that was plenty![3]

Another decision made during preproduction is whether to film each scene on a soundstage or on location. A soundstage is a huge building in which sets can be built. Shooting on a soundstage enables the production team to design and build the sets to exact specifications. It allows them to place the camera exactly where they want to put it, and to create precise scale and details in their sets.

Achieving the desired lighting is easy on a soundstage because each stage has a grid of pipes suspended from the ceiling, on which the director of photography can hang each lighting unit exactly where it should go. Also, the stage is enclosed, which eliminates noise and distractions from the outside world.[4]

Shooting on location—a real place that resembles the one in the story—usually has the disadvantage of not having enough room to spread out the necessary equipment and to move the camera freely. Generators must be brought in to supply enough electricity for the lights, and the location is more difficult to protect from outside intrusions—pedestrians, traffic and airplane noise, inclement weather—and changes in light throughout the day. Also, the cast and crew must be transported to the location, and arrangements must be made for their food and housing. However, the authentic look and feel of the location as it will appear in the movie often outweigh the disadvantages.[5] Most films require some location shooting, and some are shot entirely on location.

After the shooting of a film, it then goes through the postproduction stage, which begins with editing. The film editor, usually with the help of the director, arranges the film that has been shot into a meaningful pattern. The director always shoots far more film than is needed, and the film editor must reduce it to the usual length of a movie, which is about ten thousand, five hundred and sixty feet, or two miles. Next, the soundtrack must be placed so it exactly matches the action in the picture. When actors speak in the film, the audience should hear their voices at the same time. The musical score for the film also is added during the editing process.

It was decided that *The Sugarland Express* would be

filmed on location. In addition to Goldie Hawn, the rest of the cast had been selected, and the entire cast and crew were transported to Texas to begin production. It was an exciting time for Spielberg. He would be directing a cast of good actors, in a story of his own, and also be the first director to use a Panaflex thirty-five-millimeter camera newly developed by Panavision—a tiny camera which allowed for 360-degree panning shots, even in a small area.

The story involves Clovis Poplin (played by William Atherton), serving the last months of a prison sentence for theft, and his wife, Lou Jean Poplin (played by Goldie Hawn). She convinces him to escape and to go with her to Sugarland, Texas, to retrieve their baby, who has been placed in a foster home. Along the way, they seize a police car, and force the officer at gunpoint to drive them across Texas. They soon are pursued by other law enforcement agents. As Spielberg tells it:

> In Texas there is a posse theory. If a fellow officer is in trouble, everybody, all of his colleagues, jump into their cars and fall in behind to try and help the guy out. In this case 90 police cars were involved in a bumper to bumper pursuit that was strung out over 150 miles across Texas.[6]

When the movie was completed and released in 1974, it was this chase that received the most attention. *The New Yorker* magazine movie critic Pauline Kael wrote, "Spielberg is a choreographic virtuoso with cars.

In *The Sugarland Express*, a story written and directed by Spielberg, Goldie Hawn plays the part of a wife who urges her husband, William Atherton, to escape from jail and retrieve their child.

He patterns them; he makes them dance and crash and bounce back. He handles enormous configurations of vehicles; sometimes they move so sweetly you think he must be wooing them."[7] She also spoke favorably of his knack for bringing out young actors, and his sense of composition and movement "that almost any director might envy."[8]

Despite Kael's tribute and good reviews from other critics, The Sugarland Express did not do well at the box office. Spielberg suggested several reasons for this, one of which was marketing. The film was not released to the theater-going public until four months after the reviews appeared, and then it was allowed to play for only three weeks. Also, audiences seemed reluctant to see Goldie Hawn, known for her television performances in Laugh-In, play a role that was not light comedy.

Although The Sugarland Express did poorly at the box office, it won Best Screenplay prize at the 1974 Cannes Film Festival. At this international festival, held annually in Cannes, France, hundreds of films from all over the world are entered into competition for best film in the various categories. Much later, when The Sugarland Express was sold to television and seen by an estimated 30 million viewers, its very good rating eventually brought in a profit.

Reaching Out

Although *The Sugarland Express* had not been a box-office success, Spielberg had won the confidence of Zanuck and Brown. They immediately presented another project for him to consider. Author Peter Benchley had written the novel *Jaws*, a story of a seacoast resort town terrorized by a killer shark. Universal had acquired the movie rights, and Zanuck and Brown wanted to produce it, with Spielberg as director.

Spielberg accepted. However, since the novel needed to be adapted as a screenplay, he wanted to make some changes. He wanted the shark to appear later in the film rather than at the beginning, as it appeared in the book. As he explained, "I wanted the water to mean shark. The horizon to mean shark. I wanted the shark presence to be felt everywhere before I finally let people get a glimpse of the shark itself."[1] He also wanted to eliminate the love triangle that appeared in the book—between the chief of police, his wife, and the marine biologist.[2]

Benchley agreed to the changes, and wrote a first draft of the script for the producers and director to read. Other changes were suggested, and he wrote a second draft. When he had to leave to work on another novel, a second writer, Howard Sackler (author of *The Great White Hope*), was hired to rework the last one hundred pages. Then he, too, had to leave for another job.

It was now only four weeks before the shooting date, and Spielberg was not yet satisfied with the script. Checking into a New York City hotel in order to work undisturbed, he wrote his own 120-page version. There was still some doubt, though. Should the film's emphasis be on the shark, or on the hero who kills it?

Meanwhile, the process of preproduction was moving along. Since the film featured a killer shark, Spielberg and production designer Joseph Alves decided not to use a studio water tank, as had often been done in aquatic movies. They would shoot at a seaside location, to make the setting more real. They would also need a real-looking shark. To use an actual shark was not feasible, since they could find no Hollywood animal trainer who had trained such a large and powerful fish.

To create a life-sized replica, Robert Mattey, retired director of special effects at Disney Studios, was hired. The result was a twenty-four-foot, one-and-a-half-ton

In *Jaws*, a seacoast resort community is terrorized by a twenty-five-foot, man-eating white shark.

polyurethane shark, nicknamed Bruce. There were three versions of Bruce: The first two were designed for right-to-left and left-to-right movements on the water's surface; the third was designed for underwater filming. Each one cost approximately $150,000 to make.[3]

Alves next needed to search for a shooting location. This needed to be a picturesque seaside resort town with a sheltered bay. The bay needed to have a sandy bottom in twenty-five to thirty-five feet of water in which to submerge a twelve-ton steel platform for the shark. Other requirements were a 180-degree view of unbroken horizon, tides that rise and fall no more than two or three feet during the season, and a hotel complex reachable within forty-five minutes. The latter was needed to house and feed a film crew of over one hundred men and women, as well as the actors, producers, and directors.

Martha's Vineyard, an island off the southeastern coast of Massachusetts, was chosen for the location of *Jaws.* A popular summer resort, it is separated from the mainland by Vineyard Sound, a narrow waterway. The island is bordered on the east by Nantucket Sound, and on the south by the Atlantic Ocean—providing the wide, unbroken horizon that was needed by photography director Bill Butler.

A budget of $3.5 million was set, with the filming expected to take fifty-two days. In the spring of 1974, the entire company moved to the island. Here, with

Spielberg still uncertain about the screenplay, he hired a writer-actor friend, Carl Gottlieb, to polish the script. Even with director and writer working together, the dialogue was often not ready until the day before a scene was to be shot. The filming of *Jaws* was off to an uncertain start—uncertain because of the ocean, weather, and other difficulties that would plague the director, the actors, and the crew.

One certainty, however, was the cast of seasoned actors who were to play the leading roles: Roy Scheider would play Brody (the police chief); Richard Dreyfuss would play Hooper (the marine biologist); and Robert Shaw would play Quint (the shark hunter). Nine additional actors and actresses completed the cast.

The film opens on the fictional island of Amity, with a young woman and man at a nighttime beach party. Impulsively, she races the man down to the water for a swim, plunges into the dark sea, struggles, and disappears. Early the next morning, Brody and his deputy discover her body on the beach. She has been attacked by a shark. Immediately, Brody takes steps to install NO SWIMMING signs on the beach, but he is opposed by the mayor, who fears that this would discourage tourists from attending the upcoming Fourth of July jamboree—a major source of income for Amity.

Tourists arrive by ferry for the holiday. Despite Brody's protest, the beaches are officially opened for the season. Suddenly, a young boy floating on a rubber raft screams, and then disappears—the second victim of a shark attack. A reward is now offered to anyone who will kill the shark.

A shark is caught and killed. When Hooper, the marine biologist, examines it, he discovers that the wrong shark has been caught. This one is too small. A twenty-five-foot, man-eating white shark is still at large. White sharks are rapid swimmers, and are continually hungry. They often swim close to beaches, waiting for unsuspecting swimmers.

When yet another swimmer is fatally attacked, Brody insists that the mayor hire Quint, an eccentric, macho shark hunter. Brody, Hooper, and Quint, armed with weapons, go out in Quint's small boat to find and kill the shark. Quint brags about his harpoon method of shark killing, and ridicules Hooper for planning to use a more scientific method.

Sometime later, when the shark rams the boat and damages the engine, Quint's harpoons have no effect. Hooper is then lowered into the water in a cage, to fire a poison-tipped spear gun into the killer's mouth, but the shark rips apart the cage. When it momentarily retreats, Hooper hides in a coral reef on the ocean floor. The shark returns, destroys the boat, and devours Quint. Brody, clinging to the masthead, shoots at a diving tank that has become lodged in the shark's mouth. The explosion destroys the shark. Much to Brody's surprise,

The shark-hunter's small boat is rammed and seriously damaged by the killer shark. Aboard are actors Richard Dreyfuss (as the marine biologist), Roy Scheider (as the police chief), and Robert Shaw (as the eccentric shark hunter).

Hooper surfaces safely, and the two survivors drift toward land on a makeshift raft.

Throughout the shooting, the filming of *Jaws* was beset with problems. Only three days into the shooting, the first mechanical shark, Bruce, sank like a rock. Later, a second Bruce exploded. The cast and crew would spend hours in preparation, and five minutes into the shooting something would go wrong. The production was plagued with sudden rainstorms, strong ocean currents that separated the equipment boats from each other, labor disputes, and angry Vineyard residents. The shooting schedule dragged along from the planned 52 days to 155 days, and the original budget increased to $6 million.

Spielberg said later:

> I was panicked. . . . I was out of my mind with fear—not of being replaced, even though people were trying to fire me, but of letting everybody down. I was twenty-six, and even though I actually felt like a veteran by that time, nobody else felt that way about me. I looked younger than twenty-six. I looked seventeen, and I had acne, and that doesn't help instill confidence in seasoned crews.[4]

Finally, in September, the shooting was finished. There remained the skillful editing by Spielberg and film editor Verna Fields, and the addition of the musical score. John Williams's music became much recognized for enhancing the overall feeling of suspense and terror in *Jaws*. Said Spielberg, "His music made it another movie, made it better than I ever thought it could be."[5]

Jaws was released in movie theaters in the summer of 1975. Public response was overwhelmingly enthusiastic. Sixty million dollars was taken in during the first month. Within three months, *Jaws* became the highest grossing film in history up to that time, and earned its director $3 million.

It also earned Spielberg increased attention from film critics. Pauline Kael wrote in *The New Yorker*, "In *Jaws*, which may be the most cheerfully perverse scare movie ever made, the disasters don't come on schedule the way they do in most disaster pictures. . . . Even while you're convulsed with laughter, you're still apprehensive."[6] In the *Washington Post*, critic Gary Arnold wrote, "There has never been an adventure-thriller quite as terrifying yet enjoyable as *Jaws*, and it should set the standard in its field for many years to come."[7]

Said Spielberg about his blockbuster film, "It was an experiment in terror. It was a nightmare to shoot. I didn't have any fun making it. But I had a great time planning it!"[8]

The box-office receipts show that thousands of moviegoers had an equally "great time" seeing it.

Close Encounters

Despite the critical and financial success of *Jaws*, Spielberg had no intention of taking time off to bask in his success. During the six months of editing *Jaws* before its release, he was already writing another screenplay, which he referred to as an "adventure thriller." The story involved a friendly meeting between humans and extraterrestrials.[1]

For many years, sightings of UFOs (unidentified flying objects, often described as flying saucers), had been frequently reported in the national news. There seemed to be no scientific explanation for these reported sightings, but they created speculation among many people. Were they spaceships? Were they flown by aliens from another planet? Were they enemies planning to invade planet Earth? These questions spawned a number of extraterrestrial-invasion science-fiction films that usually depicted hostile relationships between humans and space aliens.

Spielberg objected to such a negative vision of these unknown, never-seen creatures. "In thirty years of UFO reportings, the encounters have been very benevolent," he told an Associated Press correspondent. "No sci-fi death rays, no radiation poisoning. . . ."[2]

His more receptive attitude may have been shaped by an event that took place when he was about six years old. He remembered his father rushing home in the middle of the night, bundling the family into their war surplus Jeep, and driving them to a nearby field where hundreds of people were staring up at a meteor shower in the night sky. His electrical engineer father gave the family a technical explanation of what was taking place, "But I didn't want to hear that," says Spielberg. "I wanted to think of them as falling stars."[3] This experience had so impressed young Steven that it would become the basis for a scene in the screenplay he was now writing.

Based on his long-held belief that aliens actually might be friendly, Spielberg's story involved outer space creatures landing on Earth to learn about the planet—not to destroy it. His title, *Close Encounters of the Third Kind*, may have come from the concept in a book by astronomer J. Allen Hynek: close encounters of the first kind are sightings, the second kind are physical evidence, and the third involve actual contact.[4]

In preparation for the writing of *Close Encounters*, Spielberg spent a vast amount of time researching existing information on UFOs. He read newly published accounts of sightings, and past articles in copies of old magazines. He talked with scientists, pilots, other flight personnel, government security people, and average American families. He wanted this story to be not only about UFOs, but also about people.

Spielberg's enormous success with *Jaws* prompted Columbia Pictures to take on *Close Encounters of the Third Kind*, with producers Michael and Julia Phillips, who had recently produced the successful films *Taxi Driver* and *The Sting*. A budget of eight million dollars was set, and the lengthy preproduction process began. A team of excellent filmmakers, many of whom had worked with Spielberg before, were brought together. Among them were cinematographer Vilmos Zsigmond, production designer Joseph Alves, and music director John Williams. Astronomer J. Allen Hynek, who had served as consultant to the United States Air Force on UFO sightings, was brought in as technical advisor. To bring Spielberg's special effects concepts to the screen, Douglas Trumbull was selected. He was known for doing the special effects for *2001: A Space Odyssey* and *Star Wars*, and one of his challenges would be to create a spaceship that would resemble an illuminated floating palace.

As other noted cinematographers and a large crew of

technicians were added, a search was started for the several widely different locations needed for filming. These turned out to be Devil's Tower in Gillette, Wyoming; Mobile, Alabama; the Mojave Desert in California; and Bombay, India.

The Mobile, Alabama, location was a deserted Air Force base with four large hangars. It filled the need for large buildings in which to build sets for the production. One hangar was converted into a soundstage six times the size of any available in the world. This was needed for creating a setting that would look like Indiana at night. Other hangars were used to house several smaller sets.

To protect the entire project of *Close Encounters* from being imitated, and to preserve the dramatic impact of the story until its release, Spielberg surrounded the project with a high degree of secrecy. Security guards were hired, and the cast and crew were required to present their identification badges each day before being allowed to enter a set.

With such a complex plot and with filming to be done in widely diverse locations, Spielberg kept the shooting moving forward by using storyboards. These are panels on which a series of sketches illustrate the changes of action and scene in a planned film.

Many directors use the process of storyboarding. Spielberg used it in planning the action in *Duel* and in *The Sugarland Express*. He is a visual storyteller. "I like to tell stories through pictures as opposed to telling them through dialogue."[5] "I storyboard everything. . . . I do all the preliminary sketches myself and then hire a sketch artist to do them in detail. We work it out shot by shot."[6] Spielberg feels that storyboards show him what he needs to do to get across the story points of a scene.

After finishing the writing of *Close Encounters* and storyboarding his ideas, he and production designer Joseph Alves worked together, drawing little charcoal, pencil, and crayon pictures of extraterrestrial concepts, UFOs, and landing sites. An artist then painted these ideas, after which Spielberg presented them to Douglas Trumbull. As director of special effects, Trumbull was to engineer the construction of the intricate machinery needed to carry out the various concepts.

By May 1976, the movie had been cast, preproduction was basically finished, and filming was ready to begin on location in Mobile, the base of operation.

Close Encounters opens with an international team of scientists, led by Claude Lacombe (played by the well-known French director Francois Truffaut), investigating the discovery of five United States military planes in the Sonora Desert, in Mexico. Missing for many years, they are in good condition, but are mysteriously without a crew. In the following scenes, a control tower in Indianapolis records a UFO, and in a Muncie, Indiana, home, the mechanical toys of young Barry Guiler

Director-writer Steven Spielberg sets his camera for a scene in *Close Encounters of the Third Kind.*

(played by Cary Guffey) start to move all by themselves. Also in Muncie, a power company engineer, Roy Neary (played by Richard Dreyfuss), on his way to the scene of a power failure, is scanned by a flying object. Racing home, he sees three spaceships flying past, followed by a strange small light. Other witnesses of this event are Barry and his mother, Jillian (played by Melinda Dillon). When Roy tells his wife about what he saw, she does not believe him. Shortly, his behavior becomes erratic, and he becomes obsessed with the vision of a mountain.

In Northern India, Claude Lacombe hears a vast crowd chanting a five-note sequence, and learns that the sounds were heard from the sky. A group of scientists realizes that they are receiving similar musical notes from Devil's Mountain in Wyoming. Meanwhile, when young Barry plays the five notes on his xylophone, he is kidnapped by an alien force, as his mother looks on. While watching a television newscast, Roy sees the mountain he has envisioned. He travels to Devil's Mountain, where he unexpectedly meets Barry's mother, who has been moved by the same vision. Intercepted by soldiers in chemical warfare suits, who claim that the area is being evacuated, Roy and Jillian elude the soldiers and, amid numerous obstacles, climb to the top of the mountain. Here, a huge scientific complex has been assembled. They watch as the scientists signal, with five musical notes, to a group of small spacecraft.

Suddenly, a giant Mothership appears, lands, and communicates with the Earth computers, using the five musical notes. A ramp opens on the sparkling Mothership, releasing a number of people who had been missing for years, including the air force crew from the planes in Mexico, and young Barry.

A team of scientists assemble to return to space with the aliens. Roy struggles to reach the front of the crowd. This is the chance he has been waiting for. He is led on board by the aliens, and the spaceship ascends in awesome splendor into the night sky.

The last thirty minutes of the film, with its giant, glittering Mothership and enchanting musical communication, was designed to create a sense of wonder. Said Spielberg:

> I want people to walk out of [*Close Encounters*] with more questions than they had when they walked in. I want them to consider the possibility that we are not alone in the universe, that the stars are not simply a kind of nocturnal wallpaper to be viewed indifferently. People should enjoy looking up at night, exercising their imagination a little more.[7]

The actual shooting of *Close Encounters* took five months, but the editing took a full year. During this time, the concept of the film still remained shrouded in mystery. This gave rise to dire predictions among certain people in the movie industry, particularly since the original budget of $8 million had actually reached $18

The giant glittering Mothership prepares to land on Devil's Mountain in Wyoming.

million. One financial analyst predicted in the November 7, 1977, issue of *New York* magazine that *Close Encounters* would be "a colossal flop."[8]

That same month, when it was finally released, thousands of moviegoers proved that prediction to be wrong, as did an overwhelming majority of critics. The words used most often to describe *Close Encounters* were "breathtaking," "stunning," "dazzling," "moving," and "brilliant."

The New Yorker critic Pauline Kael said of the musical communication in the final scene, "This is one of the peerless moments in movie history—spiritually reassuring, magical, and funny at the same time. Very few movies have ever hit upon this combination of fantasy and amusement. . . ."[9]

In six months, the "colossal flop" had grossed over $154 million in box-office receipts. With the triumphant success of *Close Encounters*, Columbia Pictures suggested that Spielberg make a sequel. After some thought, he suggested instead that he revise the original and make a Special Edition. The studio agreed. This gave him the opportunity to make some changes that he did not have time for in the first film. After two major sequences were added, and some scenes were deleted to propel the action, *Close Encounters of the Third Kind: The Special Edition* was released in 1980. It, too, was received with enthusiasm by moviegoers and critics.

"This new version gets another four stars," said

Pulitzer Prize-winning critic Roger Ebert of the *Chicago Sun-Times:*

> The new editing moves the film along at a faster, more absorbing pace to the mind-stretching conclusion. *Close Encounters,* which was already a wonderful film, now transcends itself; it's one of the great moviegoing experiences.[10]

Spielberg now had created two of the highest-grossing features in movie history—each with vastly different themes. His ever-active imagination was about to draw him to yet another theme.

Other Encounters

By now Steven Spielberg was totally obsessed with moviemaking, and he had acquired a number of friends, writers and directors, who shared his passion. In the 1970s, they were sometimes referred to as Movie Brats—a group of young filmmakers who combined an extensive knowledge of film and its history with an interest in technology.[1] They were the film school generation—inventive young filmmakers fresh out of the prestigious film schools that Spielberg could not get into because his high school grades were not high enough.

These young filmmakers emerged with fresh ideas of their own, and were eager to bring these ideas to a movie audience. Some already had: Francis Ford Coppola, director of *The Godfather*; George Lucas, director of *Star Wars*; Martin Scorsese, director of *Taxi Driver*; Brian

DePalma, director of *The Fury*, among others. All were enthusiastic and creative. As friends, they exchanged ideas and scripts, and talked about possible projects. They learned from each other, and were respectful of each other. Most were in their twenties, single, and as Spielberg has said on looking back, "kind of married to each other."[2]

Although the Hollywood social scene was easily available to the young, successful, single Spielberg, it had no particular appeal to him. Occasionally he dated actresses and other interesting women, but he had little interest in attending parties or other social events. He seldom took time to enjoy his success. In an interview for *The New Yorker* magazine, Spielberg admitted putting his moviemaking first at this time in his life:

> I thought that if I stopped I would never get started again, that I would lose the momentum. . . . the momentum of being interested in working. I was afraid that if I stopped I would be punished for enjoying my success by losing my interest in working.[3]

In 1976, Spielberg met Amy Irving. An ambitious young actress, she had appeared in several films directed by Brian DePalma, including *Carrie* and *The Fury*. Mutually attracted, they were immediately drawn into a relationship. However, with each on a demanding career path, it was a troubled relationship, and they finally broke up in 1980.

Meanwhile, Spielberg had launched a new project, a

comedy titled *1941*. His two back-to-back successes—a thriller and a fantasy—had given him the courage to try something different. While making *Close Encounters*, he had read the script, and could visualize it as a funny, entertaining film. The story takes place a few days after the Japanese bombing of Pearl Harbor in December 1941. It involves a group of earnest but incompetent soldiers, and their attempt to protect Hollywood from a Japanese submarine attack. Through their misplaced good intentions, the various military men, along with other characters, create madcap scenes of action-packed confusion. Included are a Japanese submarine whose captain and Nazi advisor are intent on attacking Hollywood, an American aircraft with a crazed pilot, and a general, assigned to protect the city, but consumed with watching Walt Disney's *Dumbo* at the theater. When the submarine attacks a theme park, mistaking it for Hollywood, and antiaircraft gunners fire at a radioless American plane, mass hysteria and chaos break out in the city. In the end, half of Hollywood is destroyed by its own residents, while the general, unmindful of the surrounding disaster, continues to watch *Dumbo*.

Unfortunately, the film *1941*, which was released in 1979, was not well received by either moviegoers or reviewers. At that time, America was dealing with an Iranian hostage crisis, and also with memories of its Vietnam defeat. Perhaps audiences were not too interested in seeing a war-related movie, even one labeled as a comedy. Spielberg felt that part of the problem lay in the marketing, which promoted the film as one of the funniest pictures in the world. He felt that the film was really "a spectacle, not a spectacular."[4] Also, he felt it was too noisy, explaining that if he were doing the film again, the first thing he would do would be to reduce the sound by 50 percent.

Critic Pauline Kael reported that a friend of hers, who had seen *1941*, likened it to "having your head inside a pinball machine for two hours."[5]

Spielberg's first attempt at comedy, made at a cost of $27 million, had turned out to be a crashing failure. However, it eventually recovered over $23 million and, with overseas receipts, did break even.[6] Nonetheless, this was a sobering experience for Spielberg. His way of dealing with this major disappointment was to get to work immediately making another film.

He and George Lucas had come up with an idea for an action-adventure film. As children, they had both loved cliffhanger movies set in exotic locations. They decided to do a film based on a story by Lucas and writer Philip Kaufman about a fearless adventurer they named Indiana Jones.

Paramount agreed to take on the film with Lucas as producer and Spielberg as director. *Raiders of the Lost Ark* was to be the first of an eventual three-part series, a trilogy detailing the breathtaking adventures of its superhero.

Indiana Jones (played by Harrison Ford) is an

archeologist searching for a priceless treasure in the South American jungle. After risking his life in a series of perilous adventures, he finds the treasure but is forced to give it to a rival French archeologist, and to flee from a band of plundering natives. Returning to lecture at a university, he is told by two American military intelligence agents that they have learned of the key to locating the Ark of the Covenant, the chest containing the Ten Commandments. It is believed that whoever possesses the Ark will be invincible—incapable of being defeated. Both the American government and Hitler's army are eager to recover the Ark.

The Staff of Rah (a brass medallion mounted on a length of wood) is the key to finding the Ark's exact location. It is believed that when the sun passes through the precious stone in the center of the medallion, it will illuminate the point where the Ark is buried. The Staff of Rah has been discovered near Cairo, Egypt. Indiana Jones is given the job of finding it and then locating the Ark before the Nazis do. In his search, he encounters many life-threatening adventures, as well as romance.

Spielberg, acutely conscious of his recent financial flop, finished shooting the film ahead of schedule, and at half the proposed budget, even though the film was shot on location in England, France, Nepal, Tunisia, and Hawaii. Released in 1981, it became the summer hit, and in one year took in a record-breaking $310 million at the box office.

Director Steven Spielberg setting up a shot on location for *Raiders of the Lost Ark.*

Commenting on its popularity, Spielberg said:

> It puts people in the same place that made me
> want to make movies as a child, which is wanting
> to enthrall, entertain, take people out of their seats
> to get them involved—through showmanship—in
> a kind of dialogue with the picture you've made. I
> love making movies like that.[7]

In truth, Spielberg loves making movies, no matter
what kind they are. His tremendous success as a director
had now given him the financial means to become also a
producer of films. In this new business interest, he chose
films that he wanted to see produced and be involved in,
but not always as a director. The first of these for which
he was executive producer, but not director, was *I
Wanna Hold Your Hand.* This comedy, centered around
teenagers, *The Ed Sullivan Show*, and the Beatles, was
released in 1978, about the time that Spielberg was
reshooting and reediting *Close Encounters of the Third
Kind* for the special edition. This was followed by *Used
Cars* in 1980, and *Continental Divide* in 1981.

While shooting *Raiders of the Lost Ark* in the desert
in Tunisia, he had come up with the idea of an
extraterrestrial who is abandoned on Earth and
befriended by a ten-year-old boy. Later, he discussed the
story possibility with screenwriter Melissa Mathison, and
she agreed to write the script. Universal agreed to take on
the project, with Spielberg and Kathleen Kennedy (his
longtime staff assistant) as coproducers. Spielberg, who

would direct the film, assembled an outstanding production staff and technical crew. For director of photography his choice was Allen Daviau, who had done the camera work on Spielberg's first thirty-five-millimeter film, *Amblin'*.

A major part of preproduction would be the creation of the alien from outer space, whose name would be E.T., the abbreviation of Extra-Terrestrial. Spielberg wanted "a creature that only a mother could love. I didn't want him to be sublime or beatific—or there'd be no place to go in the relationship. The story is the beauty of E.T.'s character."[8]

For this challenge, he hired Carlo Rambaldi, a special effects expert, who had crafted King Kong for that movie's 1976 remake. Rambaldi, along with hundreds of artists and technicians, created the remarkably lifelike E.T., described by one critic as "a squat, wrinkled, mud-colored beastie with a perpetual chest cold."[9] Little did its creators and film producers know that E.T. would become such a popular motion picture star.

The plot centers around E.T., who is accidentally left on Earth when his spaceship takes off. Confused, terrified, and dodging the police and scientists searching for him, he hides in the backyard of ten-year-old Elliott's home. Elliott (played by Henry Thomas) discovers E.T. and allows him to hide safely in his bedroom, where he is also protected by Elliot's sister and brother.

E.T. learns about such Earth things as television,

telephones, and refrigerators with strange food and drink. From watching science fiction films on television, he learns how to communicate with other aliens. E.T. wants to go home, but both Elliott and E.T. become ill. Elliott recovers, but E.T. appears to be dead, and scientists invade the house. As E.T. is being carried off in a van by government workers, Elliott and other children follow on their bicycles. Diverting the van attendants, the children transfer the now revived E.T. to a bicycle basket, and speed off on their bikes, pursued by police and scientists. In the forest, they meet the spaceship. E.T. joins his alien friends, and Elliott tearfully watches as E.T. waves goodbye.

When the film *E.T.: The Extra-Terrestrial* was released in 1982, it captured the imagination of moviegoers of all ages. Reviewers spoke of it as a "masterpiece," and compared it to the classic children's movie *The Wizard of Oz*. E.T., with his odd walk, expressive eyes, and attempts at imitating human speech, appealed to millions of viewers. He became so real that children even wrote letters to him—enough to be published in a book, *Letters to E.T.*

Spielberg, at age thirty-four, had made his most successful film to date, but he was not about to relax. That same year, he coproduced *Poltergeist*, based on a horror story that he described as being "all about the terrible things I did to my younger sisters."[10] (A poltergeist is a spirit that makes its presence known by

Elliott (played by Henry Thomas) and his friends desperately try to outrace the authorities in order to save E.T.

noises, knockings, and other weird happenings.) In the story, the home of a normal suburban family is disturbed by strange events. The five-year-old daughter disappears, the son is attacked by a tree, and the swimming pool is filled with writhing bodies. In the end, the daughter is returned, the family escapes from their house, and the house collapses. An effective thriller, the film drew many viewers to its scary entertainment.

Late in 1982, Spielberg began work on *Twilight Zone: The Movie*, in collaboration with three other film directors—John Landis, Joe Dante, and George Miller. Spielberg directed one of the film's four segments, "Kick the Can," about old people in a rest home rediscovering their youth. The *Twilight Zone* project was struck by tragedy when actor Vic Morrow and two small children were killed in a helicopter accident during the filming of John Landis' segment. This unfortunate incident sparked a drive for safety reform, especially for those guilds (actors and cameramen) whose members were directly involved in the filming of stunts. Although Spielberg served as coproducer of the project, he was not present at the time of the tragedy and, after investigation, he was personally cleared of any wrongdoing.[11] Released in 1983, *Twilight Zone: The Movie* received mixed reviews from critics and viewers alike.

By 1983, Spielberg needed more space in which to develop his many ideas. In gratitude for the tremendous success of *E.T.*, Sidney J. Sheinberg, now president and chief operating officer of Universal's parent organization, MCA, Inc., arranged for the building of a separate studio complex for Spielberg. A gift from Universal, it was named Amblin Entertainment, after Spielberg's early film *Amblin'*. Nestled in a far corner of Universal's lot, the complex included a Southwestern-style building with twenty-five thousand square feet of offices, editing rooms, conference rooms, and a screening room, as well as a gym, video-game room, and restaurant-size kitchen. Spielberg now had plenty of room in which to operate his own production company. Besides producing movies and television series, Amblin Entertainment would soon grow to include other enterprises such as the licensing of toys and games, and the invention of theme park rides.

From the beginning of Amblin Entertainment, Kathleen Kennedy and Frank Marshall (producer for *Raiders of the Lost Ark*) oversaw its many film projects. In his role as executive producer, Spielberg found that he often worked long hours on subjects that did not particularly interest him. More and more he began to reduce his activities as a businessperson, turning over much of this work to Kennedy and Marshall. They, in turn, shared executive producer credits on the films that Amblin Entertainment produced. Now, Spielberg had time to do what he liked to do best—direct movies.

Moving On

In the spring of 1983, Steven Spielberg and George Lucas began filming the second of their action-adventure trilogy, *Indiana Jones and the Temple of Doom*. In this story, Indiana Jones (again played by Harrison Ford), teams up in Shanghai with nightclub singer Willie Scott (played by Kate Capshaw). Seeking to trade a Manchu dynasty urn for a large diamond, Indy is double-crossed by Chinese gangsters, drugged with poison, and saved by a young boy named Short Round (played by Ke Huy Quan), who then joins Indy and Willie.

On the way to India, they survive a plane crash and a treacherous journey over wild river rapids, and they arrive at a distressed mountain village. The village had been cursed when the Maharajah (the ruling prince) stole its protective stone and its children. Determined to save the village, Indy and his companions travel to the Temple of Doom, where the Maharajah has forced the enslaved children to mine the caves for diamonds. After many narrow escapes, including one in which Willie almost becomes a human sacrifice, Indy retrieves the stone, and returns it and the children to the village.

Released in 1984 to eager movie fans, *Indiana Jones and the Temple of Doom* was immediately criticized by reviewers and parents for its excessive violence. That same year, Amblin Entertainment, with Spielberg as executive producer, released the film *Gremlins.* A combination horror, comedy, and fairy tale, this film, too, was criticized for its questionable horror.

Suddenly, Steven Spielberg's benevolent image, which had been so evident in *Close Encounters of the Third Kind* and *E.T.,* had been shaken. Public protest against films seen as unsuitable for children, with no restrictions on age, quickly led to the modification of the motion picture rating code. Adopted in 1984 by the Motion Picture Association of America, the revised code provides that a film rated PG-13 means: "Parental guidance suggested for children under age 13."[1] Spielberg fully supported this new measure, commenting that "the responsibility to the children of this country is worth any loss at the box office."[2]

One bright personal happening during the past year had been Spielberg's unexpected reunion with Amy Irving. While he was scouting locations for *Indiana Jones and the Temple of Doom* in India, she was there for the filming of *The Far Pavilions*. They met at the airport. Despite their breakup four years earlier, they were still attracted to each other, and their relationship began anew.

Meanwhile, Spielberg was engaged in a deal with NBC for a Sunday night television series, *Amazing Stories*. He had already written fifteen of the twenty-two stories needed for the first season, and would direct four of the shows.

Spielberg never seems to run out of ideas. He is happiest working on a movie set casually dressed in baseball cap, sweatshirt, jeans, and running shoes. Although he is serious about his work, he has time for a few jokes or a friendly smile for everyone on the set. When he is not directing a film, but is there as a producer, his enthusiasm seems to infect everyone he works with. Says Richard Donner, a director on the set of *Amazing Stories*, "Steven is over your shoulder the whole time. He always bows to you because you're the director, but he's got so many good ideas that you want to grab every one of them."[3]

Spielberg explains:

> I dream for a living. Once a month the sky falls on my head, I come to, and I see another movie I want to make. Sometimes I think I've got ball bearings for brains; these ideas are slipping and sliding across each other all the time. My problem is that my imagination won't turn off.[4]

About this time, Amblin's president, Kathleen Kennedy, introduced Spielberg to *The Color Purple*, a novel written by Alice Walker, for which she had won the Pulitzer Prize. Kennedy explained that it was an African-American story to which he might relate because of shared similarities in his own upbringing and Jewish heritage. "So I read the book and I loved it, but I didn't want to direct it. Then I picked it up again about a month and a half later, and I read it a second time. And I couldn't get away from certain images."[5]

Spielberg was doubtful, however, about whether he could direct this type of story. His films had always been action-oriented. This film would be more verbal; the characters would be developed through dialogue. Then he met author Alice Walker. They talked for hours, and "really hit it off."[6] They agreed on certain changes to make the story more effective as a film. They agreed on Menno Meyjes to write the screenplay based on Walker's novel. Also, they agreed on casting actress/comedienne Whoopi Goldberg in the role of Celie, one of two sisters forced to separate. At that time, Goldberg had never performed in a film, but Spielberg said later, "She turned out to be a wonderful, wonderful actress."[7]

Although he had committed himself to direct, Spielberg still had doubts as to his suitability. In his previous films, he had relied on the story to reveal the characters. In this film, the characters would tell the story. He called *The Color Purple* the biggest challenge of his career, but, he said, "I've got to do this for me. I want to make something that might not be everybody's favorite but, this year at least, is my favorite."[8]

Filming began in June 1985. Set in the rural South early in the twentieth century, the story focuses on the life of Celie, a poor African-American girl who is given by her sexually abusive stepfather to a man she refers to as "Mister" (played by Danny Glover), a brutal widower who treats her as a slave. Celie is forcibly separated by Mister from any contact with her younger sister, Nettie, the only person who loves her. Mister even intercepts and hides the letters sent to Celie. When Mister brings home his lover, Shug Avery (played by Margaret Avery), a beautiful alcoholic singer, Shug begins to slowly build a feeling of confidence and self-worth in Celie. Through Shug's efforts, Nettie's hidden letters are discovered and read by Celie. In the end, the sisters are joyously reunited, and Celie has developed enough courage to pursue happiness for herself.

Throughout the filming, Alice Walker was on the set much of the time, ensuring that the spirit of her novel was being retained. Spielberg insisted that the scene in which the sisters are cruelly driven apart by Mister be shot straight through, with no time out. He wanted the actors to feel the horror of what they were portraying. Afterward, he turned to Walker and found her in tears. "And that was good for me," he said, "because I wanted to impress her. This was her book; she'd won the Pulitzer Prize."[9]

Spielberg seemed pleased with the way the movie turned out, referring to it as "my people picture . . . not a black movie—but a movie about people everywhere."[10] He was particularly puzzled when some of the African-American community accused him of depicting African-American males as cruel sexists. Denying that the movie reinforced those stereotypes, Spielberg said, "This is a movie about the triumph of spirit—and the spirit and soul never had any racial boundaries."[11]

Critic Roger Ebert called this movie "a great, warm, hard, unforgiving, triumphant movie, and there is not a scene that does not shine with the love of the people who made it."[12] *The Color Purple* was nominated for eleven Academy Awards, including one for Whoopi Goldberg's performance as Celie.

Although 1985 had been filled with new professional projects, Spielberg had also launched a new personal project. He and Amy Irving were married, and early in June, eight days after he began directing *The Color Purple*, their son, Max Samuel Spielberg, was born. His proud father described this event as "my biggest and best production of the year."[13] Fatherhood, at the age of thirty-seven, introduced workaholic Spielberg to a completely different career, one that he apparently enjoyed. He shortened his workday at Amblin, and tried to be home at a reasonable hour; less time at work meant more time with Max. Amy called Steven "the fun parent"—the one who imitated Donald Duck and made their son giggle.[14]

At this time, Spielberg took some time off from directing movies, temporarily abandoning his long-standing plan to film a sequel to *Peter Pan*, which would have meant being on location in London, and away from his son. He did, however, direct two episodes of his *Amazing Stories* series ("The Mission," and "Ghost Train"), and he worked as executive producer on *The Goonies, Back to the Future, Young Sherlock Holmes*, and other films.

In 1986, at the 59th Academy Awards ceremony, Steven Spielberg received the prestigious Irving G. Thalberg Memorial Award, which goes to "a creative producer whose body of work reflects a consistently high quality of motion picture production."[15]

By 1987, Spielberg was ready to return to directing, and had decided to once again do a film based on a novel. *Empire of the Sun* was a semiautobiographical novel written by an Englishman, J. G. Ballard, about his childhood experiences in World War II Shanghai, China. His story of separation, survival, and the loss of innocence appealed to Spielberg. Britisher Tom Stoppard wrote the screenplay, based on the book. Most of the cast would be British. Obtaining permission to shoot in China took almost a year of negotiations. Finally, Spielberg won permission to bring a crew and

In 1986, Steven Spielberg received the Irving G. Thalberg Memorial Award from the Academy of Motion Picture Arts and Sciences. Standing next to him is Richard Dreyfuss, who presented the award.

cameras to China for three weeks. During the filming, about ten thousand extras were hired to restage the residents fleeing their besieged city.

The plot centers around a wealthy British couple and their eleven-year-old son, Jim (played by Christian Bale), living in Shanghai. In 1941, when the Japanese start bombing the city before the occupation, Jim is separated from his parents. Amid the city's chaos, he must learn to cope alone. Thrown into a prison camp, he endures cruelty, hard work, and the terror of an American air attack before being reunited with his parents several years later.

When *Empire of the Sun* was released in 1987, the film received only a mild reception at the box office. The general reaction of both critics and moviegoers seemed to be disappointment with Spielberg's serious tone. To this Spielberg responded, "I've had ten years, and a lot of success, in a certain genre of movie. Now I have to explore other forms, to shake myself out of what every artist fears, which is lethargy and apathy."[16]

Spielberg could never be accused of lethargy in his next project, *Indiana Jones and the Last Crusade*, the last of the Indiana Jones trilogy, based on a story by George Lucas. As in the previous two, the film follows the incredibly breathtaking adventures of the fearless Indy. This time the story also involves Professor Henry Jones (played by Sean Connery), Indy's father, who is kidnapped by the Nazis. The filming began in May 1988, on location in Spain, Italy, Jordan, England, Colorado, Utah, and New Mexico. Audience reaction to *Indiana Jones and the Last Crusade* was favorable, and it was considered by many to be the best of the trilogy.

Although Spielberg had been experiencing success in his moviemaking, his marriage had become increasingly shaky. Amy Irving's work took much time and hard work, as did Spielberg's, and the stress of two people frequently working on different continents put a strain on both of them. In May 1989, their publicist announced an end to their three-and-a-half-year marriage. The couple agreed to share joint custody of their son, Max, and a generous financial settlement agreement was reached. It was an amicable divorce, and through the years that followed, Irving and Spielberg have remained friends.[17]

For many years, Spielberg had been wanting to do a remake of a movie he had enjoyed in his teens, *A Guy Named Joe*. A 1943 romantic comedy, it starred Spencer Tracy and Irene Dunne. Spielberg felt that it was a reassuring story about life and about "saying it while you're here and doing it while you can."[18] A screenplay was drafted changing the original hero, a brave and reckless World War II pilot, to a brave and reckless flying firefighter in the forests of the Pacific Northwest. In the story, the hero, Pete Sandich (played by Richard Dreyfuss), is killed and returns to Earth as the phantom guardian of young pilot Brad Johnson, who falls in love

Steven Spielberg was director and producer of *Always*, a romantic comedy about a brave but reckless flying firefighter.

with Dorinda Durston (played by Holly Hunter). Dorinda, the woman that Pete had planned to marry, is still grieving over his death. Pete, as a watchful phantom, must unselfishly help Dorinda overcome her grief and find a new romance.

Always included elements of comedy, sentiment, and daredevil flying action, but it was not highly successful at the box office.

By now, Spielberg had ventured into filming several types of stories that were new to him. Perhaps the time had come to make the film he had been wanting to make for a long time.

Coming of Age

For several years Steven Spielberg had wanted to do his own version of J. M. Barrie's story of *Peter Pan*—the tale of a boy who did not want to grow up. When he read screenwriter Jim V. Hart's screenplay, *Hook*, featuring a grown-up Peter Pan, Spielberg felt this was the movie he would like to make. What interested him about this new present-day version was that it related to the many grown-ups who have forgotten what it was like to have been a child: ". . . a lot of people today are losing their imagination because they are so driven by work," said Spielberg, "and the children in the family become almost incidental."[1]

Filming was to begin in the first half of 1991, with a release date scheduled around Christmas of that same year. The film would be shot in Culver City, on the soundstage that was once used in *The Wizard of Oz*. With a budget of around $70 million, this sequel to *Peter Pan* was predicted to become one of the most expensive movies ever made. Two major expenses would be the creation of Neverland, with a lavish seventy-foot Jolly Roger pirate ship, and the casting of high-salaried actors in leading roles. Robin Williams would play Peter Banning, the grown-up Peter Pan. Also in the cast were Dustin Hoffman as Hook, Julia Roberts as Tinkerbell, and Bob Hoskins as Smee (Hook's sidekick). Glenn Close, Maggie Smith, Caroline Goodall, and others of fine talent all added to the cost of production and to the quality of the film.

The story presents the grown-up Peter Pan as a successful Wall Street businessperson who has become so immersed in his work that he shares little time with his two children. He has forgotten the joy of childhood. Reluctantly, he takes time off from work to fly to London with his family to celebrate a special tribute to Wendy Darling, the woman who had adopted and raised him years ago. In London, Peter's children are kidnapped by the notorious Captain Hook, who carries them off to Neverland. Peter cannot rescue them, because he has blocked out his memories of being Peter Pan.

With help from Tinkerbell, he is whisked back to the Island of Lost Boys. Aided by Tinkerbell and the band of orphans called Lost Boys, Peter prepares to track

Director Spielberg appears on the set of *Hook*, a sequel to the story of Peter Pan. With him are Julia Roberts and Robin Williams, who star in the movie.

down Captain Hook and rescue his children. In a duel, Hook is fatally stabbed. Peter must still win back the affection of his children, who have been brainwashed and adopted by Hook. In the process, he rediscovers his childhood and his flying skills. Thus, he regains the trust of his children, who will now have a more attentive and affectionate father.

Much anticipated by movie fans, Spielberg's *Hook* was a colorful and elaborate production, and *People* magazine did a cover story on it at the time of the film's December 1991 release.[2] In general, reviewers were not enthusiastic. However, its appeal to audiences as a family-type movie made it a commercial success. The cast seemed to enjoy making the film. Said Dante Basco, leader of the Lost Boys, "It was like coming to Disneyland to work each day."[3] The film seemed to provide a thoughtful message to four of the major participants—Robin Williams, Dustin Hoffman, Bob Hoskins, and director Spielberg—who all were dads. Hoskins (star of *Who Framed Roger Rabbit?*) told of how they would come to work and ask each other, "What wonderful story did you tell your kid last night? Did you play ball with him?" After experiencing this kind of father-competition, he said, on looking back, that he became a better father to his children than he had been.[4]

Remembering what it was like to be a child—recapturing the joy of childhood—seemed to be what

Hook was all about. In that effort, Spielberg's film could rightly be called a success.

During the filming of *Hook*, a major change took place in Spielberg's personal life. After a longtime relationship with actress Kate Capshaw, they were married in 1991. They had met when she costarred in *Indiana Jones and the Temple of Doom.*

This was a second marriage for both, and with it their family grew to include five children—one from each of their previous marriages, and three from their own. The oldest, Jessica Capshaw, age nineteen, attends a university in an eastern state. The other children are ten-year-old Max, seven-year-old Theo, five-year-old Sasha, and three-year-old Sawyer.

Spielberg's next project would be a combination of science, adventure, and terror. Writer Michael Crichton had written *Jurassic Park*, a best-selling novel about a futuristic theme park involving dinosaurs. Several studios had bid to acquire the rights to do the movie, but the sale went to Universal, where Spielberg would both produce and direct it.

Crichton then wrote the screenplay in collaboration with writer David Koepp. Preproduction started immediately and took about eighteen months. Since the main attraction would be the dinosaurs in their natural setting, constructing the huge, lifelike prehistoric animals would be a creative, time-consuming challenge. Creator Stan Winston, an Oscar winner for visual effects, agreed to accept the challenge. In his studio, a team of talented artists and engineers first went to work researching and sketching the needed animals, before the actual construction could begin.

Seven species of dinosaurs were needed, with the Tyrannosaurus rex the tallest at twenty feet. Another major character was the Velociraptor, a ferocious predator about the size of a human. Also prominent was the Dilophosaurus, actually ten feet tall, but made only four feet tall and known (in the story) for spitting a killer venom.

The animals were made movable by internal mechanisms—either computer or radio-controlled—though some body movement was managed by human performers inside the dinosaur form. To operate the enormous T-rex, however, more powerful hydraulic actuators would have to be used. In creating T-rex, an enormous form was constructed over which a layer of heavy cloth was stretched. Fiberglass covered the cloth, which was then spread thickly with clay. Between eight and ten people worked daily for sixteen weeks sculpting the huge body parts.

The setting in Crichton's novel was a remote island off the coast of Costa Rica. To resemble that setting in the movie, a remote canyon in Kauai, one of the Hawaiian Islands, was chosen for part of the shooting. The remainder of the filming would take place on soundstages at Universal Studios and Warner Brothers, and briefly in the Mojave Desert.

During much of the preproduction time, Spielberg was involved in the shooting of *Hook*, but he also was thinking about the making of *Jurassic Park* and about how he wanted to develop the various scenes. As usual, he sketched his ideas on storyboards to visualize the movement of the story. After eighteen months of preproduction work, and the completion of *Hook*, the filming of *Jurassic Park* began in August 1992.

The story centers around John Hammond, a wealthy businessperson who envisions using genetically cloned dinosaurs as an attraction for his not yet opened theme park. The dinosaur area is protected by an electric fence and an electronic safety system. Hammond invites two noted paleontologists, accompanied by Hammond's grandchildren, for a tour of inspection before opening day. (Paleontologists are scientists who study forms of life from former geologic periods, as represented by plant and animal fossils.) When a main computer blows out, making the safety system useless, T-rex knocks down the fence and starts off on a roaring rampage. All the dinosaurs run amok, crushing and devouring everything in their path. After a terrifying battle to survive, the paleontologists and children finally manage to escape from the island.

Released in the summer of 1993, *Jurassic Park* was an instant hit with theater audiences. There was some

Tim (played by Joseph Mazzello) and Lex (played by Ariana
Richards) help Dr. Alan Grant (played by Sam Neill) feed a friendly
Brachiosaurus from their perch high up in a *Jurassic Park* tree.

question, however, about its frightening effect on children. Some mental health professionals even posted warnings about the "intensity" of *Jurassic Park*'s excitement for younger children. Gerald Dabbs, a Manhattan child psychiatrist, disagreed. He believed that a part of growing up is learning to deal with stress. "It may be very painful right now," he said, "but kids will be able to come to terms with it."[5]

Jurassic Park had a PG-13 rating, and Spielberg agreed that this movie was inappropriate for children under age thirteen. He said:

> In general, though, I think children are more traumatized by violence that can be re-created in a natural setting: a movie about child abuse or a movie about murder. This is a movie that not only can't happen, but can't even be emulated. Even if audiences buy into the notion that dinosaurs are back, they still have the reassurance that they won't be attacked by a tyrannosaur on the way home. I guarantee that won't happen.[6]

Apparently not all viewers were apprehensive about the effect of a good scare. *Jurassic Park* quickly became the highest-grossing film of all time up to that moment. *Time* magazine reviewer Richard Corliss wrote that "it was the director who put the drama in every snazzy frame. For dinosaurs to rule the earth again, the monsters needed majesty as well as menace. And Spielberg got it all right."[7]

People are often curious to know what Spielberg is

like on the set. Is he strict? Is he demanding? Laura Dern, who starred in *Jurassic Park*, was asked that question in an interview with James Brady of *Parade* magazine. "It's not that he's strict," she said, "but that he's so well-prepared. He knows exactly what he wants." She thought, because of his importance, that he would set up the shot and then leave. "But he's there, like an assistant director, all the time. . . . Hanging out with the crew. We play, we laugh, we talk, then he tells us to get back to work. But he never yells."[8]

This movie mogul, who has been described as an even-tempered workaholic, does not smoke, drink, or take drugs. David Hume Kennerly, photographer for a cover story on Spielberg for *Time* magazine, wrote:

> I don't recall dealing with anybody, in government and politics or in Hollywood, who was as cooperative as Spielberg. He is a very private person who doesn't normally allow the press into his life. And he was extremely busy. But he constantly took time out for us.[9]

Steven Spielberg and his family live in a sprawling Mediterranean-style house in the Pacific Palisades area of California. In viewing Spielberg's collection of Norman Rockwell paintings, which are hung throughout the house—illustrations of traditional home and family—one might easily suspect his unspoken longing for a family-style life. His marriage to Kate Capshaw seems to have been a definite step toward establishing that kind of life. Capshaw converted from Methodism to Judaism before their marriage, saying she had long been drawn to Judaism; she liked its emphasis on the family.[10] "It was very important to me that our home be a Jewish home, that our children were raised Jewish," she said in an interview for *Harper's Bazaar* magazine.[11] Spielberg's stepdaughter, Jessica, did not convert to Judaism, but Theo, Sasha, and Sawyer will be brought up as Jews and attend Hebrew school. Max, whose mother is Amy Irving, will make his own decision when he is older.[12]

It seems clear that Kate Capshaw feels committed to Steven, to raising five children, and to managing both their California home and their home in East Hampton, New York.

Now, as a successful and wealthy family man, it appears that Steven Spielberg has come of age.

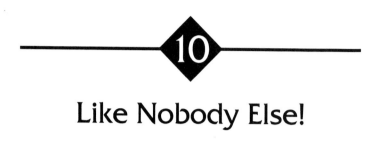

Like Nobody Else!

Despite Spielberg's reputation as the most successful filmmaker in history, many in the movie industry shrugged off his work as lacking in substance. He was considered a producer of light movies, fantasies filled with thrills and wonder. He felt that the public wanted this. He had in mind a lot of projects of a political or social nature, but he told himself:

> That's not what the public will accept from you. What they will accept from you is thrills, chills, spills, and awe and wonder. . . . I was afraid people would say, as some of them did say about both *Empire of the Sun* and *The Color Purple* . . . 'Who does he think he is?'[1]

In 1982, Spielberg read *Schindler's List*. A novel written by Thomas Keneally, it was a fictionalized account of the life of Oskar Schindler, a German industrialist who saved the lives of more than one thousand Jews during the Holocaust. As soon as he read the book, Spielberg knew that he wanted to make the film. He remembered the stories his parents and grandparents had told him. He remembered being in his grandmother's Cincinnati home when she was teaching English to death camp survivors, and how one young man showed him the number burned into his arm by Nazi officials. By twisting his arm around, he could make the number 6 turn into number 9. The trick had impressed three-year-old Steven. He was not yet aware of the tattoo's meaning.

Spielberg bought the rights to film *Schindler's List* immediately, then laid the project aside to direct *Indiana Jones and the Temple of Doom, The Color Purple, Empire of the Sun,* and other films. Also, he started his Amblin Entertainment production company. Meanwhile, Keneally's book lingered in his mind. He felt he was not ready to make the movie yet; he was not mature enough. "I had to have a family first. I had to figure out what my place was in the world."[2]

With Spielberg's marriage to Capshaw, her appreciation of his Jewish heritage, and his expanding role as a father, his life now had a balance. He was ready to make *Schindler's List.* In March 1993, while *Jurassic Park* was still in postproduction, Spielberg moved his family to be with him on location in Krakow, Poland.

The cast for *Schindler's List* involved only three key

characters, but about thirty thousand extras were hired from the local population, and Spielberg used a mostly Polish crew. Cast in the main roles were Liam Neeson as Oskar Schindler, Ben Kingsley as Itzhak Stern (Schindler's accountant), and Ralph Fiennes as Amon Goeth (Nazi commandant of a nearby concentration camp).

In the movie, Schindler, a German businessperson (a member of the Nazi party, but uninterested in its politics), aims to profit from the Nazi occupation of Poland. He buys an enamelware factory in Krakow and hires Jewish laborers, because by law he can pay them low wages. Though married, he has many mistresses and indulges himself with extravagances. With war contracts rolling in, the factory reaps enormous profits. Schindler is indifferent to his employees until Nazi atrocities against the Jews increase, and his workers are herded into a concentration camp. Suddenly, his indifference turns into compassion. When all the Jews are to be transferred to death camps, he spends his fortune to save his workers. Opening a munitions factory in Czechoslovakia, he "buys" about twelve hundred Jews for his workforce. These are the people on *Schindler's List.* By secretly providing a safe haven for them, Schindler saves these and other Jews from the gas chambers in Auschwitz.

In making the movie, Spielberg insisted on making the settings as authentic as possible. He used the narrow streets in Krakow's old Jewish quarter, the actual entrance to Schindler's factory, and even the apartment where he once lived. When he was not allowed to shoot a sequence inside Auschwitz, he built his own set outside the camp. Except for brief scenes at the beginning and at the end, and the scenes involving a little girl's red coat, the entire movie was shot in black and white to resemble the documentaries and photos from that period.

Almost every day of the company's three months in Poland, it rained or snowed, adding to the somberness of the filming. Because of the subject matter, there was none of the lighthearted bantering that usually takes place between scenes. Spielberg had anticipated this, but had not expected so much sadness every day:

> It didn't ever seem to any of us that we were making a movie. It always seemed like we were re-creating something absolutely and utterly indescribable, horrendous. And so the days were spent in deep, deep sadness.[3]

Nevertheless, Spielberg found a great personal satisfaction in having made *Schindler's List*. "This has been the best experience I've had making a movie. I feel more connected with the material than I've ever felt before."[4] The connection was with the stories he had heard of his relatives who experienced the horrors of that period.

At over three hours, *Schindler's List* was longer than the average movie. Spielberg had no illusions about recovering the $23 million cost of production. Profits were not anyone's motives in this project: "'I'

On location in Poland, Steven Spielberg directs *Schindler's List*, starring Liam Neeson (right) as Oskar Schindler, who saved the lives of more than eleven hundred Jewish workers sheltered in his factory.

this film for myself, for the survivors, for my family—and for people who should understand the meaning of the word 'Holocaust.'"[5]

Although Spielberg did not have high box-office expectations, the reaction to *Schindler's List* was immensely favorable. *The New Yorker* film critic Terrence Rafferty wrote:

> It is by far the finest, fullest dramatic (i.e. nondocumentary) film ever made about the Holocaust. And few American movies since the silent era have had anything approaching this picture's narrative boldness, visual audacity, and emotional directness.[6]

Maclean's reviewer Brian D. Johnson wrote, ". . . an undeniably powerful drama . . . by dramatizing the Holocaust with such vividness and scale, Spielberg has helped to pass its lessons on to future generations."[7] Early in March 1994, after the movie's premiere in Frankfurt, Germany, the daily *Frankfurter Allgemeine Zeitung* told its readers on the front page, "Everybody should see this film. It forces the viewer to ask why others didn't try to do what Oskar Schindler managed."[8]

Within the movie industry, there was much speculation about who would win the Oscars this year at the Academy Awards ceremony. Although Spielberg had been nominated three times as Best Director (for *Close Encounters of the Third Kind, Raiders of the Lost Ark,* and *E.T.*), he had never won. Many in the film community felt that he had been unfairly spurned by the Academy. This year, *Schindler's List* had won both the New York and the Los Angeles Film Critics Award, and two weeks before the upcoming Academy Awards, Spielberg won the coveted Directors' Guild trophy. Perhaps, this would be his year.

On the evening of March 21, 1994, an air of excitement and suspense surrounded the hundreds of people at the Dorothy Chandler Pavilion in Los Angeles. An estimated one billion viewers throughout the world would be watching this much-awaited event. Throughout the evening, *Schindler's List* had already won Oscars in five categories. The time had come to announce the winner for Best Director; the Oscar went to Steven Spielberg. The audience stood applauding as the winner sprinted onto the podium. Then, a beaming but thoughtful Spielberg accepted his Oscar, saying, "To the six million who can't be watching this, among the one billion watching this telecast tonight, thank you."[9] His mother, Leah Adler, wept as she watched her son receive his first Oscar ever. His wife, Kate Capshaw, said, "I've been waiting so long to give him a standing ovation at an Oscar show."[10]

With one award yet to be announced, there was little doubt that the winner of Best Picture would be *Schindler's List*, and it was. Now, on this night, Steven Spielberg had the rare honor of being the Best Director of the Best Picture: like nobody else!

Steven Spielberg stands with his mother, Leah Adler, and wife, Kate Capshaw, after receiving Oscars for Best Director and Best Picture at the 1993/66th Annual Academy Awards.

In the weeks that followed, Spielberg was much in demand for interviews by the media. The question most frequently asked was "What are you going to do next?"—to which he replied that he had no idea what to do next, but felt he could treat himself to some time off. The idea sounded logical, but it did not last.

The favorable reaction of moviegoers to *Schindler's List* brought higher box-office receipts than expected. With his share of the profits, Spielberg immediately formed a foundation, Survivors of the Shoa, to record a visual history from firsthand accounts of the Holocaust survivors. (*Shoah* is the Hebrew word for Holocaust.) The goal is to gather thirty thousand interviews for a global archive. Through Survivors of the Shoa, volunteers are being trained to interview survivors, not only in the United States, but also in Canada, France, Israel, and Australia, as well as in other countries. "By this time next year," says Spielberg, "we will have 200 camera crews in the field every single day, seven days a week." He calls this project "the most gratifying experience of my entire life."[11] These videotapes will be made available to researchers at five centers, including the United States Holocaust Memorial Museum in Washington, D.C.

Spielberg's ideas seem to flow nonstop. He is not ¹⁻ an outstanding movie director, but through this he has also become a successful n September 1994, *Forbes* magazine

100

reported that the financing of a Spielberg movie works somewhat like this: The studio pays for all costs, including production, advertising, and distribution. Once the finished movie begins bringing in revenue, Spielberg gets 5 percent if he produced the film, and 15 percent if he directed it. This cut of the revenue can grow to 30 percent, until the film breaks even. Then Spielberg and the studio split the profits 50-50.[12]

Both his creativity and his business sense have made Spielberg a billionaire at age forty-six. This has enabled him to delve into other business ventures, such as his deep-sea diner, Dive!, in Los Angeles. Co-owned with his friend Jeffrey Katzenberg, their $7 million restaurant specializes in more than twenty different varieties of submarine sandwiches. Decorated to look like a submarine, it also provides Spielberg-type special effects. Every forty-five minutes, the restaurant seems to submerge, as video monitors flash footage of an undersea dive. A second Dive! opened in Las Vegas in June 1995, and other units are expected to open in the future.

In October 1994, Spielberg revealed another business venture. Jeffrey Katzenberg (a former Disney Studio executive), David Geffen (a record executive), and Spielberg were creating a new studio. This three-way partnership, named DreamWorks SKG, would focus on providing multimedia entertainment, including motion pictures, animated films, television shows, and recorded

Jeffrey Katzenberg, Steven Spielberg, and David Geffen at a news conference on October 12, 1994, at which the formation of their multimedia studio, DreamWorks SKG, was announced.

music. In March 1995, DreamWorks SKG announced that it would add a line of computer software to its multimedia venture. This software will be produced by the Microsoft Corporation under the name DreamWorks Interactive. Another of Spielberg's business interests is the television show *ER*, a popular weekly medical drama. His Amblin Entertainment coproduces the show, and Spielberg critiques the scripts.

Meanwhile, Kate Capshaw managed to fit a movie into her already full schedule of child-rearing, home management, and being the wife of superactive Spielberg. In the legal thriller *Just Cause*, released in early 1995, she plays the female lead, Lori Armstrong, a former district attorney. Capshaw is selective about the parts she takes, and she shares those decisions with her husband. "Steven and I are partners, and our life together is our production."[13]

In all of his ventures, it is believed that Steven Spielberg will never stray too far from his own directing of films. In March 1995, at a dinner of the American Film Institute, he was presented the Life Achievement Award.

Spielberg's heart is in making movies—either directing, writing, or producing. Says he, "The only time I feel totally happy is when I'm watching films or making them."[14] Millions of moviegoers hope that Steven Spielberg will feel "totally happy" making films for a long time.

Chronology

1947—Steven Spielberg born in Cincinnati, Ohio, on December 18.

1960—Wins contest for short war film, *Escape to Nowhere*.

1964—*Firelight* shown for one night at Phoenix movie theater.

1965—Graduates from Saratoga High School; parents divorce.

1967—Attends California State University at Long Beach.
-1969

1968—Produces and directs short film, *Amblin'*.

1969—Receives contract to direct Universal Studios television series; *Amblin'* wins awards at film festivals.

1973—First full-length film, *Duel*, released.

1974—*The Sugarland Express* released.

1975—*Jaws* released.

1977—*Close Encounters of the Third Kind* released.

1979—*1941* released.

1980—*Close Encounters of the Third Kind: The Special Edition* released.

1981—*Raiders of the Lost Ark* released.

1982—*E.T.: The Extra-Terrestrial* and *Poltergeist* released.

1983—*Twilight Zone: The Movie* released; Universal Studios builds Spielberg a moviemaking complex, Amblin Entertainment.

1984—*Indiana Jones and the Temple of Doom* released.

1985—Marries Amy Irving; son Max Samuel born; *The Color Purple* released.

1987—*Empire of the Sun* released.

1989—Spielberg and Amy Irving divorce; *Indiana Jones and the Last Crusade* and *Always* released.

1991—Marries Kate Capshaw; daughter Sasha born; son Theo adopted; *Hook* released.

1992—Son Sawyer born.

1993—*Jurassic Park* and *Schindler's List* released.

1994—Receives Oscar as Best Director for *Schindler's List*; establishes Survivors of the Shoa; forms DreamWorks SKG.

1995—Receives Life Achivement Award.

The Films of Steven Spielberg

As Director

Duel (1973)

The Sugarland Express (1974)

Jaws (1975)

Close Encounters of the
Third Kind (1977)

1941 (1979)

Close Encounters of the Third Kind:
The Special Edition (1980)

Raiders of the Lost Ark (1981)

E.T.: The Extra-Terrestrial (1982)

Twilight Zone: The Movie (1983)

Indiana Jones and the Temple
of Doom (1984)

The Color Purple (1985)

Empire of the Sun (1987)

Indiana Jones and the
Last Crusade (1989)

Always (1989)

Hook (1992)

Jurassic Park (1993)

Schindler's List (1993)

As Producer/Executive Producer:

I Wanna Hold Your Hand (1978)

Used Cars (1980)

Continental Divide (1981)

Poltergeist (1982)

Twilight Zone: The Movie (1983)

Gremlins (1984)

The Goonies (1985)

Back to the Future (1985)

Young Sherlock Holmes (1985)

The Money Pit (1986)

An American Tail (1986)

Innerspace (1986)

Batteries Not Included (1987)

Who Framed Roger Rabbit? (1988)

Back to the Future II (1989)

Dad (1989)

Back to the Future III (1990)

Chapter Notes

Chapter 1

1. Emanuel Levy, *And The Winner Is* . . . (New York: Continuum, 1991), p. 31.
2. Joel Siegel, "Oscar Overview," ABC *Good Morning America*, transcript 2027, March 22, 1994, p. 1.
3. Charles Gibson, "Steven Spielberg Interview," ABC *Good Morning America*, transcript 2027, March 22, 1994, p. 4.

Chapter 2

1. Julie Salamon, "The Long Voyage Home," *Harper's Bazaar*, February 1994, p. 136.
2. Ibid.
3. "Orthodox Judaism," *Random House Webster's College Dictionary* (New York: Random House, 1993), p. 955.
4. Dianne M. MacMillan, *Jewish Holidays in the Fall* (Hillside, N.J.: Enslow Publishers, 1993), pp. 8–9.
5. Salamon, p. 136.
6. Denise Worrell, "The Autobiography of Peter Pan," *Time*, July 15, 1985, p. 62.
7. Salamon, p. 136.
8. Worrell, p. 62.
9. Ibid.
10. Richard Corliss, "I Dream for a Living," *Time*, July 15, 1985, p. 57.
11. Worrell, p. 63.
12. Ibid.
13. Dan Olmstead, "Ex-Boy Scout Makes Movies," *USA Weekend*, July 28–30, 1989, p. 4.
14. Corliss, p. 57.
15. Ibid., p. 56.
16. Ibid., p. 57.
17. Philip M. Taylor, *Steven Spielberg: The Man, His Movies, and Their Meaning* (New York: Continuum, 1992), p. 58.
18. Worrell, p. 63.
19. Stephen Schiff, "Seriously Spielberg," *The New Yorker*, March 21, 1994, p. 106.
20. Salamon, p. 186.
21. Diane K. Shah, "Steven Spielberg, Seriously," *Los Angeles Times Magazine*, December 19, 1993, p. 66.

Chapter 3

1. Philip M. Taylor, *Steven Spielberg: The Man, His Movies, and Their Meaning* (New York: Continuum, 1992), p. 61.
2. Diane K. Shah, "Steven Spielberg, Seriously," *Los Angeles Times Magazine*, December 19, 1993, p. 26.

3. Richard Corliss, "I Dream for a Living," *Time*, July 15, 1985, p. 57.
4. Taylor, p. 48.
5. Judith Crist, *Take 22: Moviemakers on Moviemaking* (New York: Continuum, 1991), p. 358.
6. Ibid., p. 359.
7. Corliss, p. 56.

Chapter 4

1. Judith Crist, *Take 22: Moviemakers on Moviemaking* (New York: Continuum, 1991), pp. 363–364.
2. Ibid., p. 364.
3. Ibid.
4. "Motion Picture," *The World Book Encyclopedia*, (Chicago: World Book, Inc., 1992), p. 852.
5. Ibid.
6. Philip M. Taylor, *Steven Spielberg: The Man, His Movies, and Their Meaning* (New York: Continuum, 1992), p. 82.
7. Pauline Kael, *For Keeps* (New York: Penguin Books, 1994), p. 559.
8. Ibid.

Chapter 5

1. Philip M. Taylor, *Steven Spielberg: The Man, His Movies, and Their Meaning*, (New York: Continuum, 1992), p. 87.
2. Judith Crist, *Take 22: Moviemakers on Moviemaking* (New York: Continuum, 1991), p. 367.
3. Donald R. Mott and Cheryl McAllister Saunders, *Steven Spielberg* (Boston: Twayne Publishers, 1986), p. 35.
4. Steven Schiff, "Seriously Spielberg," *The New Yorker*, March 21, 1994, p. 107.
5. Taylor, p. 87.
6. Pauline Kael, *For Keeps* (New York: Penguin Books, 1994), p. 691.
7. "Steven Spielberg," *Current Biography Yearbook 1978* (New York: H. W. Wilson Co., 1978), p. 402.
8. Taylor, p. 89.

Chapter 6

1. Donald R. Mott and Cheryl McAllister Saunders, *Steven Spielberg* (Boston: Twayne Publishers, 1986), p. 54.
2. "Steven Spielberg," *Current Biography Yearbook 1978* (New York: H. W. Wilson Co., 1978), p. 402.
3. Philip M. Taylor, *Steven Spielberg: The Man, His Movies, and Their Meaning*, (New York: Continuum, 1992), p. 56.
4. Pauline Kael, *For Keeps* (New York: Penguin Books, 1994), p. 754.
5. Taylor, p. 29.
6. Ibid., pp. 49–50.
7. "Steven Spielberg," p. 403.
8. Ibid.
9. Kael, p. 755.

10. Roger Ebert, *Roger Ebert's Movie Home Companion: 1991 Edition* (Kansas City, Mo.: Andrews and McMeel, 1991), p. 100.

Chapter 7

1. Donald R. Mott and Cheryl McAllister Saunders, *Steven Spielberg* (Boston: Twayne Publishers, 1986), p. 1.

2. Steven Spielberg interview, "American Cinema," PBS, February 27, 1995.

3. Stephen Schiff, "Seriously Spielberg," *The New Yorker*, March 21, 1994, p. 107.

4. Judith Crist, *Take 22: Moviemakers on Moviemaking* (New York: Continuum, 1991), p. 375.

5. Pauline Kael, *For Keeps* (New York: Penguin Books, 1994), p. 870.

6. Philip M. Taylor, *Steven Spielberg: The Man, His Movies, and Their Meaning* (New York: Continuum, 1992), p. 20.

7. Simon Glickman, "Steven Spielberg," *Newsmakers: The People Behind Today's Headlines* (Detroit: Gale Research, Inc., 1993), p. 463.

8. Mott and Saunders, p. 111.

9. Ibid., p. 110.

10. Richard Corliss, "I Dream for a Living," *Time*, July 15, 1985, p. 54.

11. Mott and Saunders, p. 134.

Chapter 8

1. Donald R. Mott and Cheryl McAllister Saunders, *Steven Spielberg* (Boston: Twayne Publishers, 1986), p. 87.

2. Ibid.

3. Richard Corliss, "I Dream for a Living," *Time*, July 15, 1985, p. 56.

4. Ibid.

5. Philip M. Taylor, *Steven Spielberg: The Man, His Movies, And Their Meaning* (New York: Continuum, 1992), p. 113.

6. Ibid., p. 114.

7. Ibid.

8. Corliss, p. 61.

9. Taylor, p. 116.

10. Ibid., p. 115.

11. Ibid., p. 118.

12. Roger Ebert, *Roger Ebert's Movie Home Companion: 1991 Edition*, (Kansas City, Mo.: Andrews and McMeel, 1991), p. 105.

13. Corliss, p. 54.

14. Ann Bayer, "Spielberg—Husband, Father, and Hitmaker," *Life*, May 1986, p. 148.

15. Academy of Motion Picture Arts and Sciences, *Rules*, p. 5. Information courtesy of Kristine Krueger, Legal Rights Coordinator.

16. Taylor, p. 123.

17. Stephen Schiff, "Seriously Spielberg," *The New Yorker*, March 21, 1994, p. 108.

18. Taylor, p. 123.

Chapter 9

1. Philip M. Taylor, *Steven Spielberg: The Man, His Movies, and Their Meaning* (New York: Continuum, 1992), p. 117.
2. Jeannie Park, "Ahoy! Neverland!" *People*, December 23, 1991, pp. 92–96, 99–100, 102.
3. Ibid,. p. 95.
4. Ibid., p. 102.
5. David Gelman, "What's So Bad About a Little Trauma?" *Newsweek*, July 12, 1993, p. 66.
6. Richard Corliss, "In Jurassic Park, Steven Spielberg Has a Monster Movie With a Lot of Bite," *Time*, June 11, 1993, p. 70.
7. Ibid.
8. James Brady, "In Step With: Laura Dern," *Parade Magazine*, October 23, 1994, p. 14.
9. John A. Meyers, "A Letter from the Publisher," *Time*, July 15, 1985, p. 6.
10. Stephen Schiff, "Seriously Spielberg," *The New Yorker*, March 21, 1994, p. 108.
11. Julie Salamon, "The Long Voyage Home," *Harper's Bazaar*, February 1994, p. 191.
12. Ibid., p. 188.

Chapter 10

1. Steven Schiff, "Seriously Spielberg," *The New Yorker*, March 21, 1994, p. 98.
2. Lois Grunwald, "Steven Spielberg Gets Real," *Life*, December 1993, p. 52.
3. Joel Siegel, "Oscar Overview," ABC *Good Morning America*, transcript 2027, March 22, 1994.
4. Andrew Nagorski, "Spielberg's Risk," *Newsweek*, May 24, 1993, p. 60.
5. Ibid., p. 61.
6. Terrence Rafferty, "A Man of Transactions," *The New Yorker*, December 20, 1993, p. 112.
7. Brian D. Johnson, "Saints and Sinners," *Maclean's*, December 20, 1993, p. 51.
8. Andrew Nagorski, "Schindler's List Hits Home," *Newsweek*, March 14, 1994, p. 77.
9. Laurin Sydney, "Schindler's List Tops Oscar Awards," *Showbiz Today*, CNN transcript 504, March 22, 1994.
10. Laurin Sydney, "Oscar Winners and Celebrities After Award Show," *Showbiz Today*, CNN transcript 504, March 22, 1994.
11. Laurin Sydney, "Spielberg Works to Preserve Holocaust Survivor History," *Showbiz Today*, CNN transcript 656, October 28, 1994.
12. Randall Lane, "I Want Gross," *Forbes*, September 26, 1994, p. 104.
13. Michael J. Bandler, "A Star is Reborn," *Chicago Tribune*, February 12, 1995, sec. 6, p. 6.
14. "Steven Spielberg," *Current Biography Yearbook 1978* (New York: H. W. Wilson Co., 1978), p. 404.

Further Reading

Corliss, Richard. "I Dream for a Living." *Time*, July 15, 1985, p. 57.

Crist, Judith. *Take 22: Moviemakers on Moviemaking*. New York: Continuum, 1991.

Ebert, Roger. *Roger Ebert's Movie Home Companion: 1991 Edition*. Kansas City: Andrews and MacNeel, 1991.

Kael, Pauline. *For Keeps*. New York: Penguin Books, 1994.

Mott, Donald, and Cheryl McAllister Saunders. *Steven Spielberg*. Boston: Twayne Publishers, 1986.

Nagorski, Andrew. "Spielberg's Risk." *Newsweek*, May 24, 1993, p. 77.

Salamon, Julie. "The Long Voyage Home." *Harper's Bazaar*, February 1994, p. 136.

Schiff, Stephen. "Seriously Spielberg." *The New Yorker*, March 21, 1994, p. 107.

Shay, Don, and Joy Duncan. *The Making of Jurassic Park*. New York: Random House, 1993.

Taylor, Philip M. *Steven Spielberg: The Man, His Movies, and Their Meaning*. New York: Continuum, 1992.

Worrell, Denise. "The Autobiography of Peter Pan." *Time*, July 15, 1985, p. 62.

Index